AF575747

Translated by GAO YUBING

# ALWAYS,
# OWNED BY WHAT WE OWN

WANG JIANWEI

ACC ART BOOKS

## CONTENTS

# PREFACE

Consider swimming as an example. When I jump into the water, I become part of it. Water allows me to float on its surface so that the trees, stones and sands by the shore can see me. I tread water while water laps me. We interact with each other: water is both the object and the medium – it could hinder me or turn me into a part of its background.

This type of interrelationship forms the basis of this world. Water turns me into one of its objects, just like fish, insects and invisible microorganisms living in it; it was not created solely for humans to swim in, but it allows humans to develop a skill.

In today's world, this may imply that any impactful action necessarily involves more participants. I am unable to use any existing taxonomies to define the situation I am in, as I am trapped in the situation. While I interact with all these objects, I can neither rank them in advance (because such a ranking system only makes sense to us), nor reveal the so-called truth about any of them. I can only learn about, collide and interact with them – these timeless objects – without the comfort of saying that I understand them.

Besides, I am not certain that an object I see – a piece of wood, a twig, a piece of tin or a bottle of glue – is 'deciding' the fate of the next object. Different versions of the future exist in my hands, as well as each of these objects' hands; no version in any of the hands could replace another. Henceforth, I cannot even declare that I understand my job and the 'work' this job has created. If a piece of 'work' is a holistic experience, then the holisticness has disappeared.

An organism may interact with countless objects. What is shaping the course of this action? This shall definitely become a new collective action. I try to avoid omission or, to put it another way, I try to present this collective mass as fully as possible, rather than cherry-picking a few items that seem to assert impact, such as enhancing, diminishing, taking emergency measures during unexpected changes, and presenting them as evidence. How did these happen? I try to recall the circumstances under which they happened rather than simply supplementing with theories or words, because I can neither translate their thoughts nor judge them.

In the end, this new collective mass is splendid yet strange. They cannot join a gathering or demonstration like us, but they can look at each other. Often, these objects and I jostle and tumble with each other, avoiding the invasion of one another's space with our bulkiness, while giving way to and righting each other, so that all can flow freely. All these naturally grown animals – you may call them plants – are different from 'nature'; they have grown in places least expected by us; so much so that when we see them, we are at a loss. We are obliged to say, let’s just call it art.

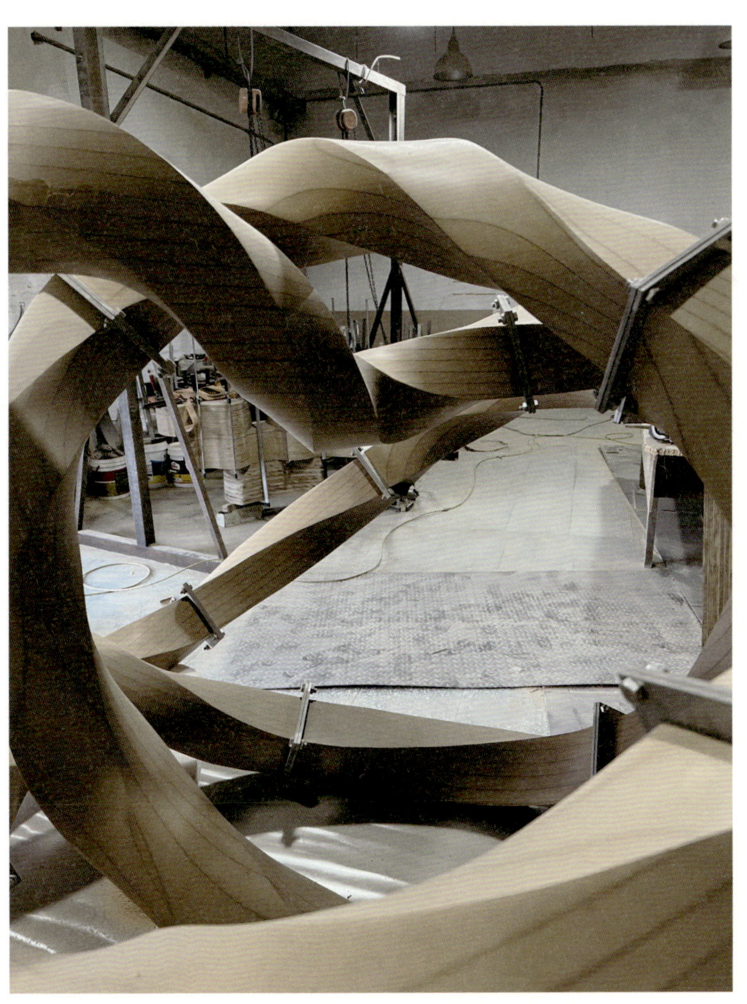

*Things are fluid and multifarious. They are not chosen; they are not commodities stuffed in a shopping bag. They are simply laid out there. Laying out comes before choosing; there is no 'connection' among various layouts, which are incongruous. Such fluidity cannot dictate the environment in which it exists.*

# CHAPTER 1

## COUNTERPART IS OMNIPRESENT

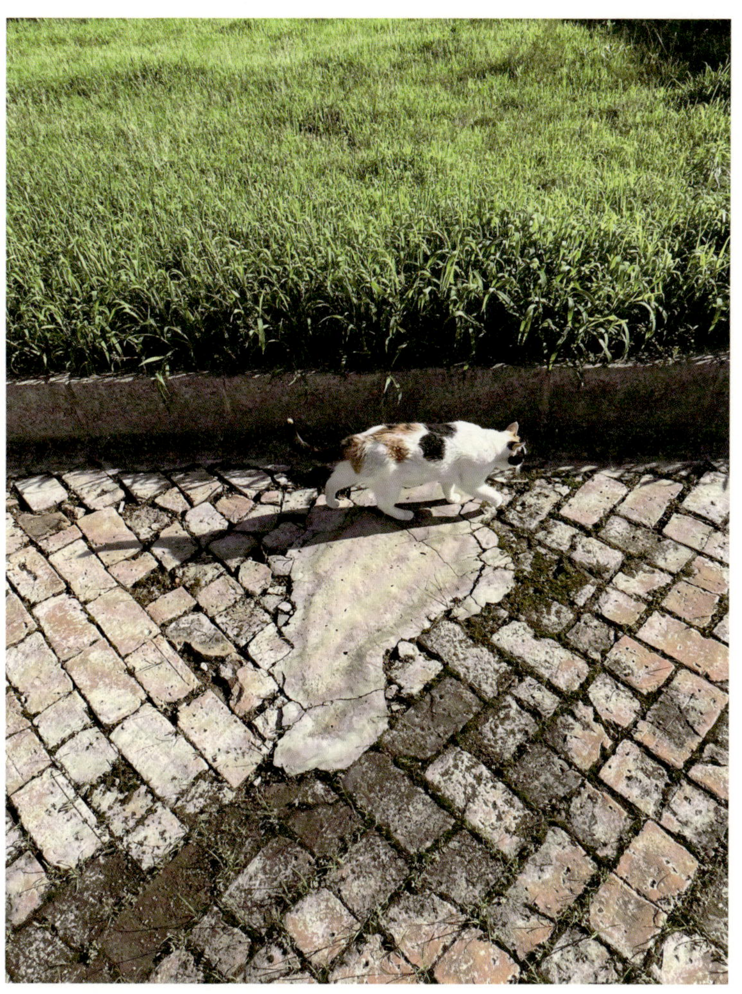

*Plants performing photosynthesis under 41°C and a cat walking on the ground that is hot and humid: they are simultaneously moving on different sides of the pavement. Even before I used my mobile phone to capture the image, a more universal, causal relationship had already existed between them. They were squeezed into the frame of my phone. Light intensified heat, the camera boosted the energy; the screen enabled the creation of art.*

## ASYMMETRY

The fire extinguisher has expired. It was 'betrayed' by a piece of paper hanging from it. In the past, I have only imagined a scenario in which an extinguisher would be used: when a fire unexpectedly breaks out, following the instructions on the user's guide, I first turn the extinguisher upside down, then pull out the safety valve and press hard on the switch. White foam is ejected. Such knowledge came partly from some random notice on a wall around town, some window display or some diagram, and partly from scenes of firefighters in action in various disaster movies. I have never really used a fire extinguisher; therefore, I have never encountered its expiry. Even though my brain stores such knowledge and memories, I cannot synthesise them into an actual experience.

Slavoj Žižek once noted the connection between supermarket food and the expiry dates on the packaging. He used it as an example to illustrate the relationship between the Real and the Imaginary in Jacques Lacan's sense. However, the expiry date of the extinguisher does not cause any theoretical confusion for me, but an anxiety, which has arisen from a sense of losing control over the things I have been familiar with. From that moment on, new boundaries were established between me and my surroundings, especially the environment that I used to work in on a daily basis. Things once within my reach seem to have come to life, attempting to move away from their original positions – the fridge, the safety socket, the charger, the tap and the paint thinner have all become potential points of explosion. All of them used to be defined by their 'expiry dates' and were hidden in a place far away from my understanding of 'validity periods'. Now they are no longer items defined by my consciousness but beyond my understanding.

The replacement of an expired extinguisher does not put my mind at rest, even though the problem has been solved. On the contrary, as I searched for more items that have expired, I had to reconnect with the things that had once been familiar to me, using a different approach. Before, most of the time when I interacted with them, I would have understood how to handle them first. Their usefulness depended largely on how effective they were, and rarely on their expiry dates. That is to say, I used my own eyes to decide whether they were effective. An 'expiry date' not only touched upon the potential effectiveness of an item, i.e., it being no longer useful once removed from its proper position, but also reminded me of things that I could have overlooked in an environment deemed familiar to me, i.e., items that I failed to pay attention to, given their seeming familiarity.

The first issue that reconnecting brought about was that I had to confront myriad things. Before, I seemed to have known how to use them like the back of my hand. But now the concept of 'expiry' is pushing this boundary and I have to start all over to understand these objects that I come into contact with. The best approach for continuing this interaction is to list out in the form of a work schedule the items that I will need to use every day: the grey door of my studio (two fire extinguishers next to it have been removed), the cracked cement ground, the weeds that have grown out of the cracks – when they are stepped on, a strange smell emanates from the point of breakage – the cat, the compressor of the air conditioner, the diagram that the computer is generating, the paint colour-chart, the receipt for the emulsion, and so on. I made the list according to the chronological order of my encounters. They have never been dragged into any category before, such as environmental, architectural, natural and cultural, or according to whether they are useful to me; nor have they been classified based on certain principles, such as art (culture, artistic work), industrial output (by corporates, by society), taxes or country systems. They have lost their original interrelationship as well as the meaningfulness and the value established and sustained by such a connection.

Validity and expiry are decisions that we impose on objects. When they break away from the rules that we set for them, they are liberated. Such freedom allows them to exist in a 'flatness' (in the sense of the philosophical theory of Flat Ontology) that is based on equality. I become part of this world – just one thing among many. On one hand, flat ontology breaks the chains of comparison. The latex paint is no longer juxtaposed against the paint brush. The return key on the computer and the fruit, the air conditioner and the business licence – they have established a new network, what Bruno Latour terms 'actor-network'. This allows many nonhumans to join and form a new collective.

The chair, the penalty demand notice and the TV news about a volcanic eruption have been re-collected and re-ordered. Their possible expansion cannot be helped and, to a large extent, I have no control over this new ordering. On the other hand, when we place these things on an equal footing to ourselves by implementing flat ontology, their meaning expands and a multiplicity is created. They are liberated from the old order and are free to form any order (any 'beingness'), just as we are. For example, the cat.

A cat wandered from my neighbour's rooftop into my studio. Initially, he did it out of hunger, but after he was fed, he decided to stay. The first question we had was: what to call him? We were soon able to take the moral high ground with our adoption of the cat. However, this sense of moral pleasure seemed so cliché. A visitor called him a 'stray cat', which immediately implied that the cat was associated with social characteristics; that is to say, once we call him a stray cat, we have changed the cat and the environment – he is no longer just an animal but an object of the environment. By rushing into a societal interpretation of the cat, we effectively strip away its characteristics as an animal and define him only by his social characteristics. At this point, the cat finds itself in a very vulnerable position, where other forms of knowledge quickly come into play. For example, sociologists might use this as a case study to learn about the area – population, income distribution, pet adoption rate and living environment, as well as the correlations among these factors; ethicists are concerned about why animals are abandoned in the first place and henceforth humans' attitude towards animals; biologists view cats as living creatures and focus on their gender, age and sterilization. The cat gets mired in various relationships when viewed through different lenses, but the characteristics of the animal itself seem to be overlooked. The cat cannot be fully defined by these relationships. As an animal, he hunts down mice, climbs trees, catches sparrows and leaps off roofs. Such characteristics are completely independent of our perspectives of him. The initial idea that he is a stray cat fades into the background.

Martin Heidegger classified objects into the twin categories of 'present-at-hand' and 'ready-to-hand'. He took a hammer as the object of analysis: when being used – held by the carpenter as a tool to fix a nail or used on a construction site – the hammer is an object 'ready-to-hand'; when not in use – laid on the table, for example – the hammer becomes 'present-at-hand'. However, the most important part of Heidegger's famous analysis of tools is that, if the hammer was broken or damaged, functions that had never been considered would soon reveal themselves and we would notice what had previously been hidden in the background and overlooked.

As for the extinguishers, I used to come across them almost every day. Whether it was windy, rainy or hot, I had never noticed them because they were 'ready-to-hand' – always around but never taken note of.

The philosopher Graham Harman's take on Heidegger's analysis of tools is rather original. In Harman's view, Heidegger had understood the way we interact with objects. At first, we are not aware of the objects because we are using them but not paying attention to them. It is only when an object breaks, that it 'emerges from its shadowy underground of pure competence and reveals its contours to view. If the city suddenly loses electrical power, if I should begin to cough uncontrollably, I am rudely reminded of entities previously taken for granted'. Just imagine, if I walked past those extinguishers, whether they had expired or not, would I interact with them more or less?

Nevertheless, the concept of 'expiry' changed my mind about the extinguisher because I now noticed it as a characteristic of the extinguisher. Even though it had always possessed this characteristic, it was just a piece of information that only occasionally appeared in my consciousness. If it was captured in an image, it was only the fire and scenes of burning that appeared in my imagination; even though such an image was vivid, and even full of passion, it was just my consciousness. Neither was I ever asked and nor did I try to satisfy my visual desire and experience it in real life. As a result, I never truly owned that extinguisher, even though it was right there.

Originally, I would first classify the items, then make a choice that was one-sided and based on my preferences. Such unbridled freedom existed only in my subjective will and ignored all external objects. However, when things didn’t turn out the way that I wished, I stopped believing in them. Through the new way, I accept the simultaneity of 'chosen' and 'to choose'; through the idea of 'expiry' and the modification of the use of the instruction manual, I learned to keep on learning about things, and not just simply use them in a 'correct' manner. I put my 'thoughts' in a suitable place.

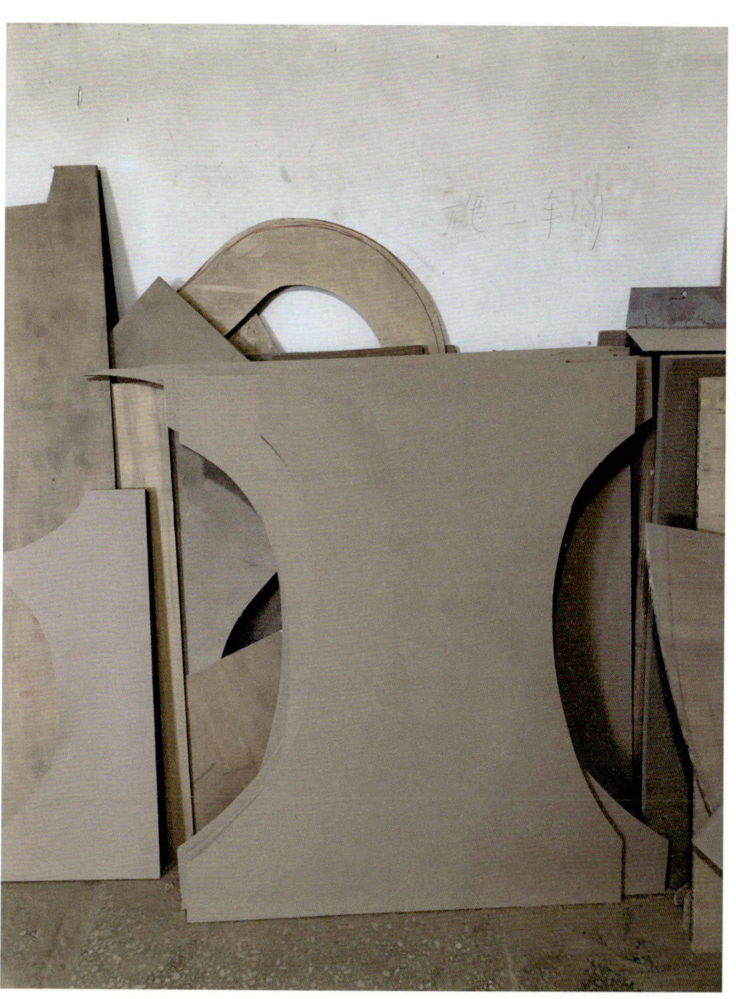
施工车间

*Things piled up in a corner or laid before my eyes are not specially catered to me. Before, I probably took things such as explosion-proof equipment, a rain shelter, a manhole cover, and so on, as 'my' things to handle; but after the 'expiry' episode, I realised that there was another 'instruction manual' for them. Before these things entered my consciousness, they had already existed: 'isolated' in the yard, on display in the window of a hardware shop or on a stall of construction materials in a market. They were used in different ways by different people, without feeling any sadness or caring about who the user was.*

## MANG ZHONG (GRAIN IN EAR)

In Southern China, before Mang Zhong, wheat is harvested, river water poured into the field and seedlings of rice planted instead, the field turning green overnight. From a geological perspective, all living and non-living things are unique sensors that receive and interpret information from the outside and the inside, participating in and facilitating the changes of the environment together. Such facilitation sometimes manifests as the striking patch of green but is sometimes hidden from us, just like a seedling being buried in the soil. Seedlings are not the only living things in this environment – along with weeds, spores, bacteria, all sorts of wiggling microorganisms, and the soil, they form a complex, symbiotic environment. Moreover, when we zoom in to look closely at the surface of the seedling, we see a group of bacteria break the cellular walls and tiny worms crawl all over the germ. However, this is not an invasion because the seedling rightly embraces its 'enemy'. Various members of the environment are constantly involved in the process of restructuring, destruction and repair, with each individual trying their best to survive while simultaneously supporting the environment with their survival. Such complex, invisible processes of interaction have no clear boundaries.

After Mang Zhong, farmers will discard the excess rice seedlings into the river, letting these 'useless' plants drift away with the water, like some sort of ceremony.

At the same time, those seedlings that are planted will look the same until they flower and their ears grow long. However, the grain after Mang Zhong has not yet completed filling, leaving them with long strings of empty shells.

That's the way they evade our understanding of nature. Agrilogistics over tens of thousands of years has not completely tamed these plants as they 'fake' their growth in response to our domestication – empty shells are beyond our limited understanding of nature and self. However, it is the disappearance of only the fruit but not the real world – or one could say, it's the disappearance of the point of symmetry between our cognition and the reality. Yet, before such a disappearance occurs, we are exposed at a place where the subject and the world have no overlap. The empty shells become a new object.

Mang Zhong is nature's metabolism. Mang Zhong and I are both in the process of metabolism. This change of nature, this solar term, has become a new object that sets me, my work, partners, tools and materials in a process of changing. I am sculpted by Mang Zhong; the materials (a type of engineered wood called Oriented Strand Board, or 'OSB') and the tools that I use correct my 'past', i.e., they use existing logic to deduct changes, use cause to control result. My 'future' is constantly edited. Photosynthesis has changed the colour of the surface of the earth through chlorophyll; through symbiosis, seedlings in the soil have created a new metaphor. In this metaphor, Mang Zhong, OSB and I have all become objects.

After Mang Zhong, the colour of OSB has undergone some changes, with its density fluctuating as a result of the change in season and air pressure. Consequently, it breaks down more easily, becomes more ‘friendly’ to the tools with just the right level of density, so that dust will not stick to the saw blade during cutting and it is not as fragile as before. Subsequently, this leads to a change in the wood's volume and the frequency of its change.

Through a series of repeated interactions between the boards and the saws, the emulsion glue and F-clamp, a new image has been forged, thereby taking up a new space or, shall we say, territory. Furthermore, it has become plural, a new object with its own home.

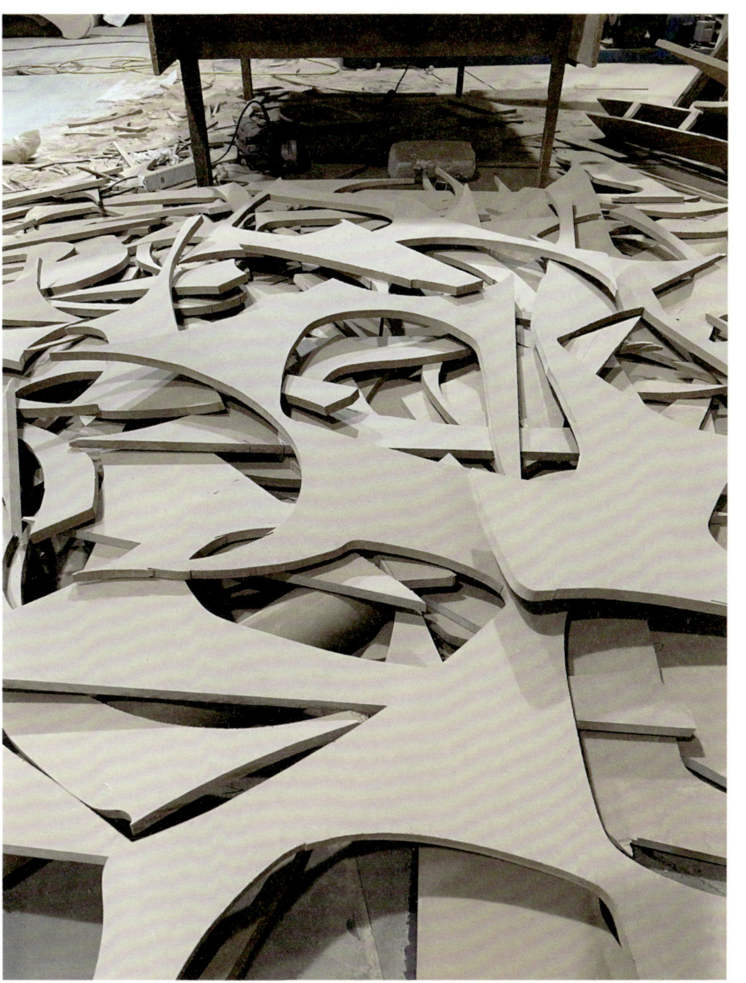

*It is not control or 'complete' dominance, nor is it a random collage. All is wrapped in the presence of a gigantic object. Your movement is limited. The artist's work includes reducing the scope for explanation by words and the degree of 'subjective feelings'.*

## IT AND THEM

During summer, when the rainy season approaches, all animals become restless, as if waiting for the first clap of thunder. The thunder breaks the dullness of winter and takes away the dry weather of spring. Animals start to move around, pieces of wood expand, tools get rusty, paper and linen become mouldy. Perhaps the animals' ancestors all coincidentally came from the sea, so humidity makes them ecstatic, as if it's a carnival that they have been anticipating for a long time. The thunder leaves behind mould and rust – such is their refusal of dryness; humans paint, preservatives and dehumidifiers acting as refusals of their refusal.

Mould and rust are like animals in action – they move fast and work together; they were born in the same place, but they like to roam around. The mouldy fungus floats around in the air, sometimes landing on the back of a cat or the shell of a crawling bug. They infiltrate inside the cracks of the wood and under the handle of the toolbox. They like to settle down in humid places and multiply at an astonishing speed, nestling in the creases of the canvases and the uneven surfaces of the nails. Most of these groups do not have any obvious characteristics or fixed territories. How much of fluidity depends on my preferences? I can only react and respond. When I confront them, they at once expand aggressively and remain peacefully in their own environment, reproducing as the wind blows.

In this scenario, more than anything, I am imagining. Perhaps the act of art is just a form of reaction, therefore the so-called 'imagination' of the artist doesn't really exist. To be more precise, the artist cannot prove that this feeling is special because it extends to the artist's entire surroundings: countless messages received via the computer, plenty of novels, the stupid and creepy images that appear on mobile phones, the invasion of the art supplies by those covert microorganisms, the growth of mould under humid conditions, the appearance of creases as a result of expansion and the cracks given dry conditions; each of them has a role to play and I am unable to ascertain the function of each in the overall effect on me. Such an influence was collectively asserted by these multiple factors. Our reaction to it also becomes part of the overall equation that cannot be calculated – it is not simply a sum of parts, but some accumulative effect of one object on another. However, I am only conscious of my own feelings.

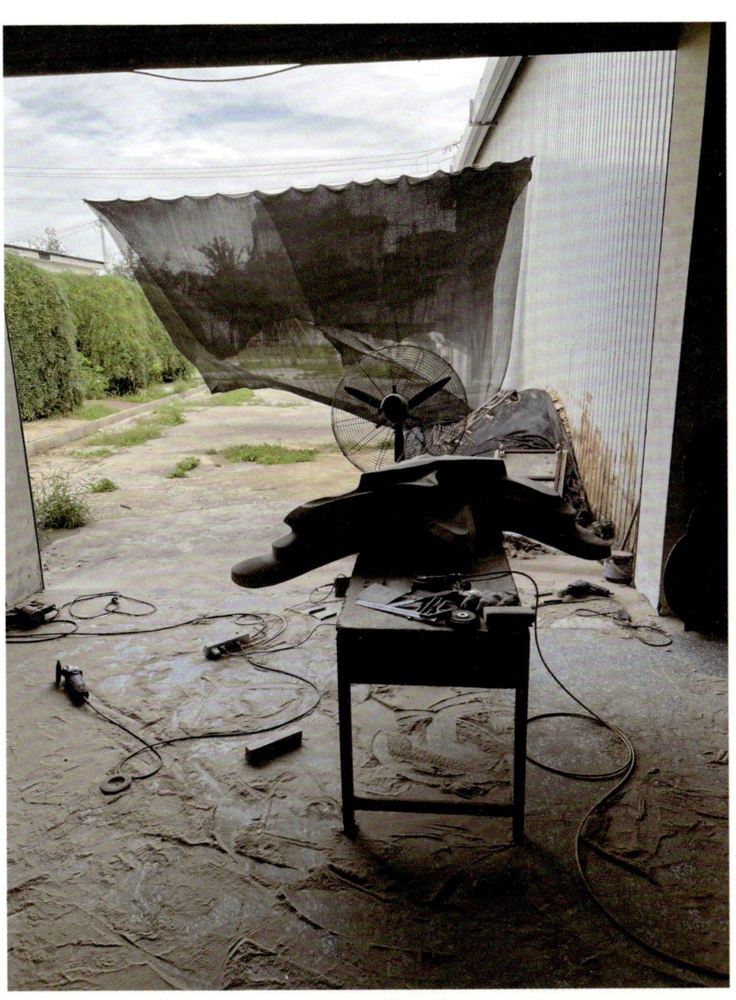

*Before being turned into the artist's raw materials, the steel plates, OSBs and wooden planks had always been materials and had different meanings for their existence. They embody memories and exist in a timeframe between yesterday and today.*

# CHAPTER 2

# ALWAYS, NOT COMPLETELY

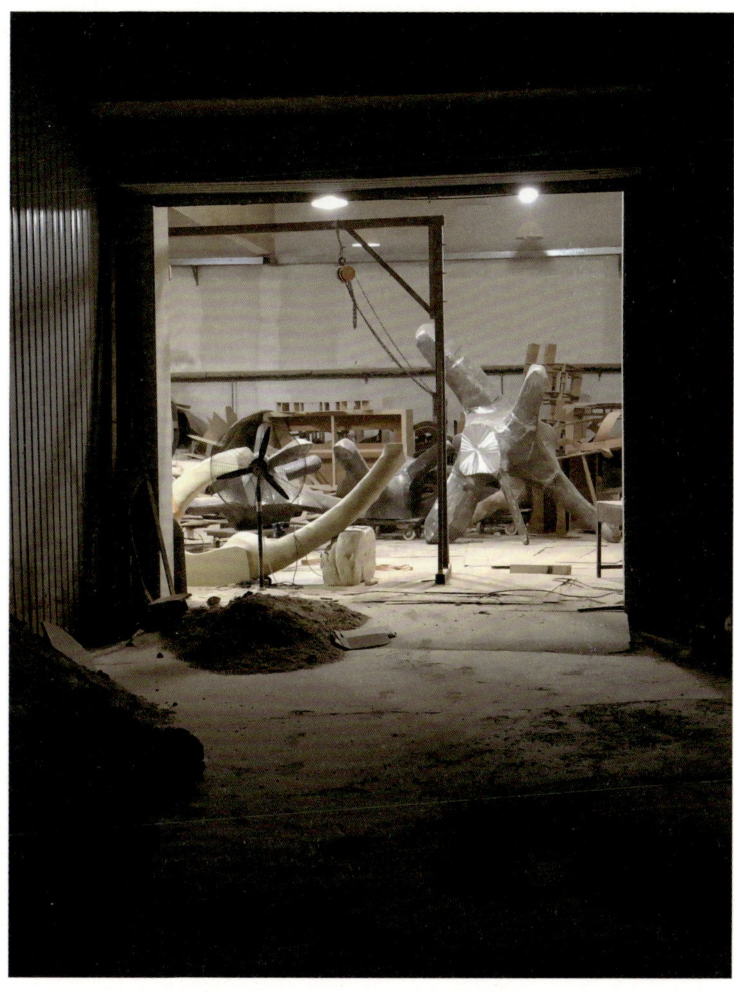

*Very often (it happens too many times, so it has become difficult to count or remember), all we do is make a choice. So-called skimming through, listening, talking and reading is all done in preparation for the choice. However, in most circumstances, a choice is always between 'I love' and 'I completely detest'. There is a huge gap in between, hence there are too many things that we can choose from. A choice or a decision sometimes only eliminates one of them. Whichever way it goes, it feels unfinished.*

*Smart phones and digital media have redefined our freedom of choice. We can send nine pictures in one go. These nine pictures that have been granted permission or chosen are all but one thing out of many, only appearing on one screen. As to why these images appear at this particular date and time, we are not clear; it is somewhat bewildering. Therefore, to a large extent, what had meaning at the time the images were taken, has now become meaningless. Possibilities are hidden and unchanged.*

## A CASE OF INTENSIFICATION

During the final stage of spray painting, the entire piece of work is hung in the air to minimise its contact with the supporting platform and to ensure the quality of painting. We temporarily set up support structures to provide reinforcement while minimising contact with the artwork. Such supporting structures are mostly random materials, chosen without any consideration of their appearance, only for their functionality. They come in mass and seem humble in volume and form when compared to the artwork they support. However, the day arrives when the artwork is moved away. All of a sudden, they present themselves side by side, scattered around in an orderly manner, just like miniature pagodas on the dusty ground. Each procedure that has taken place – spray painting, polishing, water-based painting and coating – is visible on their surfaces, too. As a result, they have become so plump and exquisite. I am so pleasantly surprised by all these and yet, they are completely indifferent.

This is very much like the Chinese saying of 'Unintentionally planting willows, yet they grow lush'. But we have ignored a hidden truth – willows do not grow naturally to create shade; even though someone planted them without the intention of creating shade, the action of planting was still done by a person. There is a gap between unintentional and natural. To put it simply, it's still a human action and the consequence of the action is the intervention by a human in nature's territory, which leads to the creation of 'willowy shadow'. What was originally a human action is rhetorically altered as if it were nature taking its course. The Chinese saying is described in such a way as to create the impression that humans unintentionally follow the laws of nature, thereby creating a new vision.

However, such an unethical human intervention also creates something new. Perhaps many years later, at the spot where the willows were planted, there will be patches of willowy shade, thereby changing the original ecological environment. At the roots of the trees, the soil is growing something new – a new chain of vegetation has emerged. Together with the 'indigenous species', the new plants have to adapt to the sudden changes in the environment. The relationship between the natural environment and the growth of a plant is broken; the plant goes through changes itself and has changed the surroundings to eventually grow in a different way, becoming part of the true nature.

Real intensification cannot be predicted or stated beforehand; the future of things is not completely in our control. However, we have some influence; we casually carry out a plan until it becomes no longer fortuitous. It is a result of both the foreseeable and the unforeseeable. It only demonstrates that we haven't yet figured out the driving force behind the process, or perhaps there is no driving force at all. Nevertheless, we can take the next step since we have reached a consensus over instability.

Only with instability can we see the normality we are in. We are not independent of each other; we may become fragile any time we encounter others, such as, but not limited to, strangers, friends, pets and many other nonhumans (I often get isolated by my external organ – mobile phone). Instability exists precisely because of these factors that are 'not me and not controlled by me'. Instability intensifies our seeking help from others (for example, I rely on screen time more than ever), while asking us to reflect on our counterfactual illusions – the belief that we can live independently. Those others, too, are subject to their own instability as well as the instability between them and others.

Where do they occur? What are their trajectories, locations and processes?

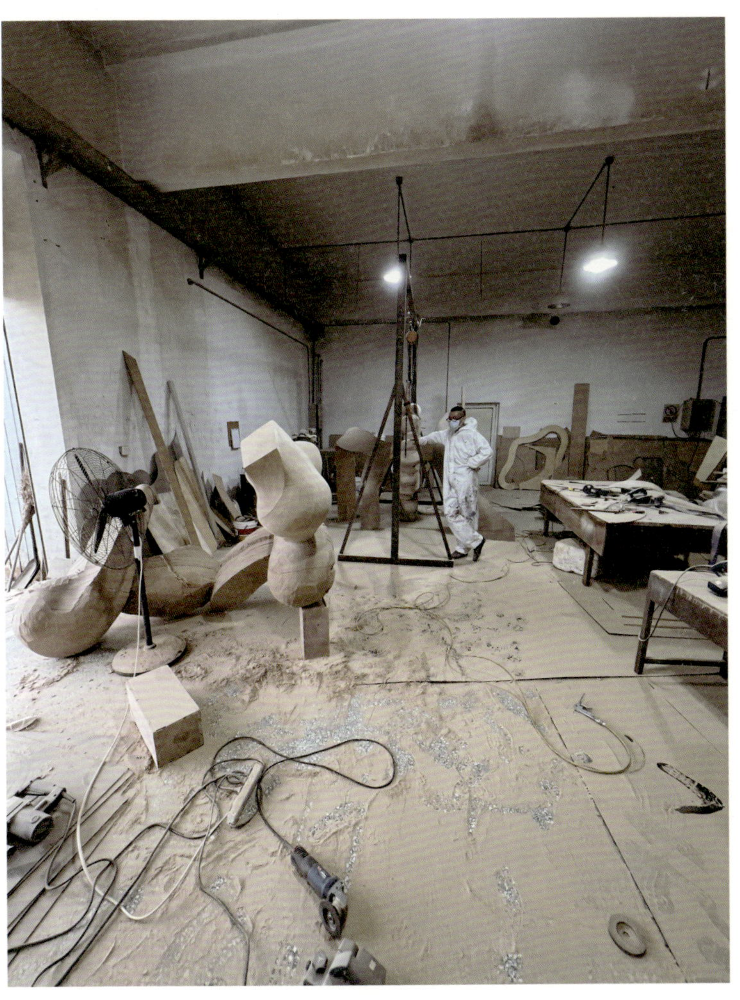

*Art and artists both exist in this world of ours. Artists interact with many objects in the world; any kind of classification is a decision made by human beings only. Artists must first break away from the alienated subject of human being.*

As such, I divert my attention to a work scene, and not just work itself.

I take the studio as an object. Me being part of the object, my focus is no longer merely on the artist and his behaviour, but the more complicated intertwining relationships between people and things, as well as those among different things. The willing and the unwilling participants are not here to just satisfy the functional needs of human beings. When I shift my focus to the studio, a place that is simultaneously subject to repetitive routines and unforeseeable changes and accidents, I learn to pay attention to all the participants in the process. It is a new collective, with no boundaries or frameworks as originally imposed, but situated in a new environment. Just like an archaeological site, the 'natural objects' that used to cover the surface are slowly removed to reveal the hidden traces of time. The key is that the participants no longer take the roles assigned by human – you, the person next to you, the electric drill, the warm wood and the stainless-steel plate are not just 'objects' decided by me, the 'subject', but also objects with their own histories and processes.

# SAW THEM BEFORE I DID

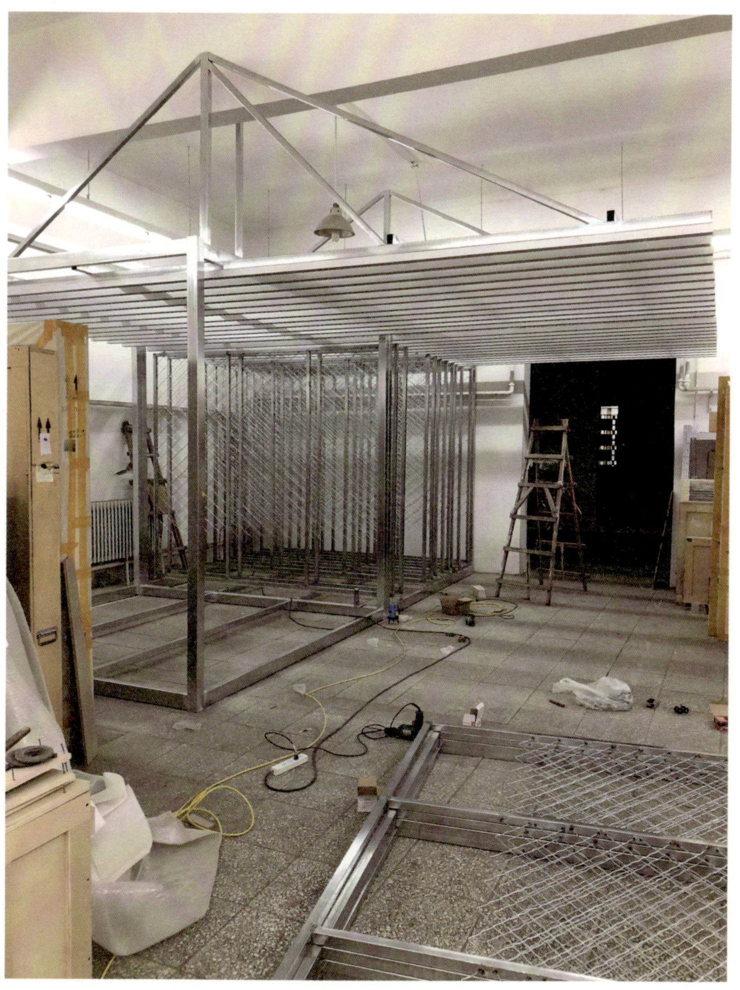

*Among numerous causal relationships, the relationship between the work I am doing and myself is just one of many and is unnamed. I am unable to preestablish a causal relationship just because I wish to. None of the interactions I have with any materials could be predetermined as a form of art. This is probably because, in such interactions, causal relationships are not solely artistic.*

*For example, I can be called a subject, an object, an organism, a user, a client, Party A or Party B. In everything that I am involved in, all the characteristics of my identities are involved. Moreover, such interactions happen in real life, and are not to be quantified by statistics. Once fixed, those terms, identities and their relationships may all be translated into culture – realities governed by culture.*

Actually, when the polisher touches the wood and generates a piercing noise, most other things are simultaneously at work but drowned out by the noise of polishing. However, even without this noise, I rarely pay attention to other things. This has nothing to do with our consciousness – our consciousness has been trained to be associated with consciousness. During this time, or at the working site, while I focus my attention on the polisher and the wood, other things are wrestling and colliding about at the same time: the electric wire is connected to the plug, never asking where electricity comes from; the dust on the wood is absorbed by the fan; the base that ensures the polisher works properly is fixed on the ground and endures even greater pressure than the polisher via the user's weight, which is passed along through his hands holding the base. A few days later, the base will be redecorated and appear in a different place. In addition, given the ceiling height and the size of the window, the working condition is reasonably good – even the flow of the air is dismissing the decibels to avoid harmful effects on the human body. I cannot completely understand how and with what parameters things are worked out in order for the work of 'making art' to proceed, but I can still use them. Of course, I can apply some theory to this work or completely omit 'this part' altogether. Yet, what is the basis and the context of 'this part' that allows these other things to share this moment with me?

I can certainly attempt to use different areas of knowledge to explain the work at hand – from the perspectives of scenes, effects and processes. I can take any angle and the difference is the starting point, which hinges on the tool I use. Art history takes the part out of its context and describes its characteristics in great detail, establishing how it is 'different from the rest', so as to attain certain artistic value. However, before a part is temporarily cut off from the whole and isolated, it was functioning as a part of the whole, in order for the whole to present itself as such. Therefore, 'a certain part' is used and is never in a state of 'not in use'. Another way is critical intervention, which does not believe in what is 'present' at all. This line of thought comes from nowhere (which is a characteristic of critique) – everything may very well just be sending us signals. Another explanation uses 'feelings' to describe it: by defining the rust on metal as 'traces of time' or 'invasion of the environment', or by using it as a contrast to an unnatural concrete jungle, or as a way to provide spiritual comfort to people whose bedrooms are built with cement. This type of 'feeling' turns metal and stone into subjects for the study of humanities. However, even before we start to use metal and stone, they had a previous function before we began using them. A stone shows its natural power not because we make use of it, but because it embodies power from the beginning. Our interpretation of the stone, from its implication to its symbolism, only happens in our brains, not to the stone itself. This battle between human brain and everything else has no winner. We feel frustrated because we think everything is waiting to be named by us, just like in the army: only when the commander calls out a name, will that soldier respond. The identity of everything is confirmed only if we name it. We treat things like human beings; whether it's a tree or a stone, they only come alive when we look at them. Those lively trees and grasses are silently waiting in the world for our call; without us calling, they are useless materials.

It is only at that moment in the studio that the 'materials' present themselves in front of me. My choice to use any particular 'material' could be based on certain stories but I actually have no clue about them. This should be the starting point of the so-called work of art. Yet, we sometimes spend too much time projecting concepts onto them, before and after. We are very much like a long-distance runner who is standing at the starting line, covered in gear and focused on getting to the finishing line smoothly. It is difficult to take any step forward with the full load. Likewise for art: it doesn't happen before the beginning; hence the beginning is a kind of liberation – an acknowledgement that it's a thing. In philosophy, it's called noumenon. We should acknowledge this reality as it is, not by how we talk about it.

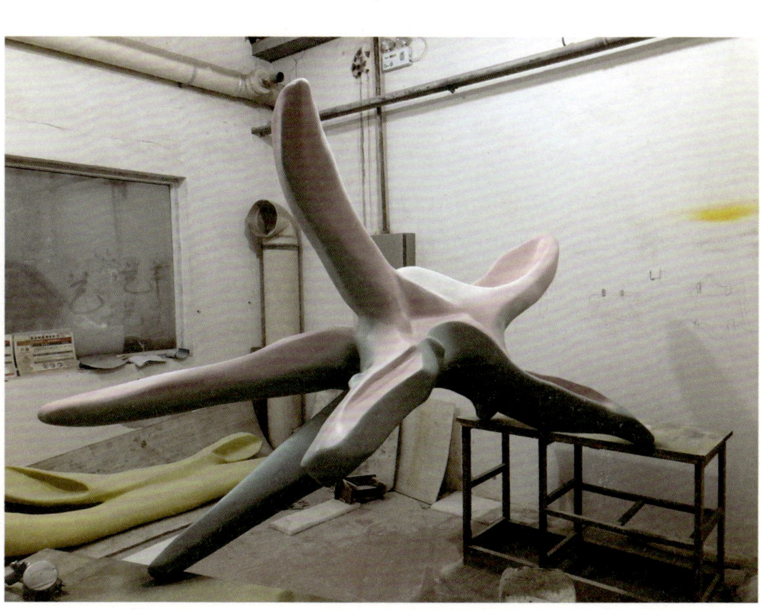

*Wood, drill, tartrazine and me – each of us is given an identity. However, apart from the designated identities, there exists another type of ecological system – the interactions among organisms, individuals, fibres, metals and chemical elements. All of them, including me, form new causal relationships which exist before our identities and names are established. Art is one of the causal relationships.*

# REALITY AND 'REALITY'

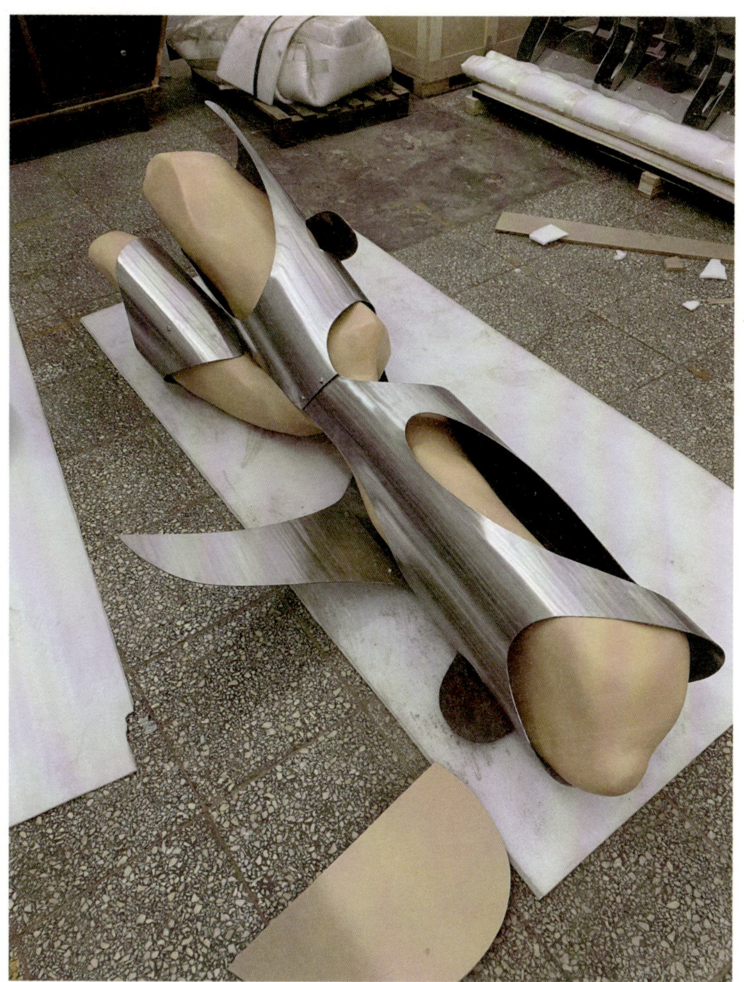

*Too many things happen in secrecy because no one is looking, and there is no time to deal with what is happening, so it can only remain in darkness.*

We still have time to reconsider this reality – the gulf between reality through media and actual reality is so wide. I am constantly dealing with reality but am never able to properly describe it. On one hand, it appears in my work – be it just the wood itself or the wood 'identified' as one of the materials. On the other hand, it is bound by the hurdles in communication, either because the way of communication is limited or because there is no need to pass along any message. However, in difficult situations such as these, things emerge with new energies. Very often, no detailed instruction manual is available to clearly illustrate this reality; words cannot replace it. This reality could only be hidden, probably because of its constraints. But that doesn't lead us to Ludwig Wittgenstein's conclusion, in which he says to stay silent in the face of the unspeakable. Because the reality, or the actuality, of art is never part of language training and practice. No matter how much we respect Wittgenstein, it doesn't compel us to stay silent at the wrong time. It is not unspeakable but untouchable. Speaking and describing are uses of language around the reality but not around the entity.

At all stages of my work, from the beginning to the end (including painting, sculpture, installation and video), I have to confess that the artist could never fully understand the object. At most, it's limited to an understanding of the 'materials', but even that understanding is partial. For example, apart from the difference in thickness, 5mm and 3mm steel plates are different in their characteristics as 'materials'. As an object, it still hangs in the air. Hence, I am able to discover something new about it during my unlimited interaction with it. No practice is ever pure or 'innocent'. 'Doing it with my own hands' doesn't necessarily endow spirituality to the object. On the contrary, all movements of my body and hands are defined by the relationships between people and things. All the objects that I use for practice – their existence 'in darkness', their interaction, absorption and engulfing – are just like the symbiotic relationships between cells and are never accomplished through the theories and practices of human beings.

Art is just like a biosphere whereby evolutionary symbiosis always happens beyond my consciousness. Always, but not wholly.

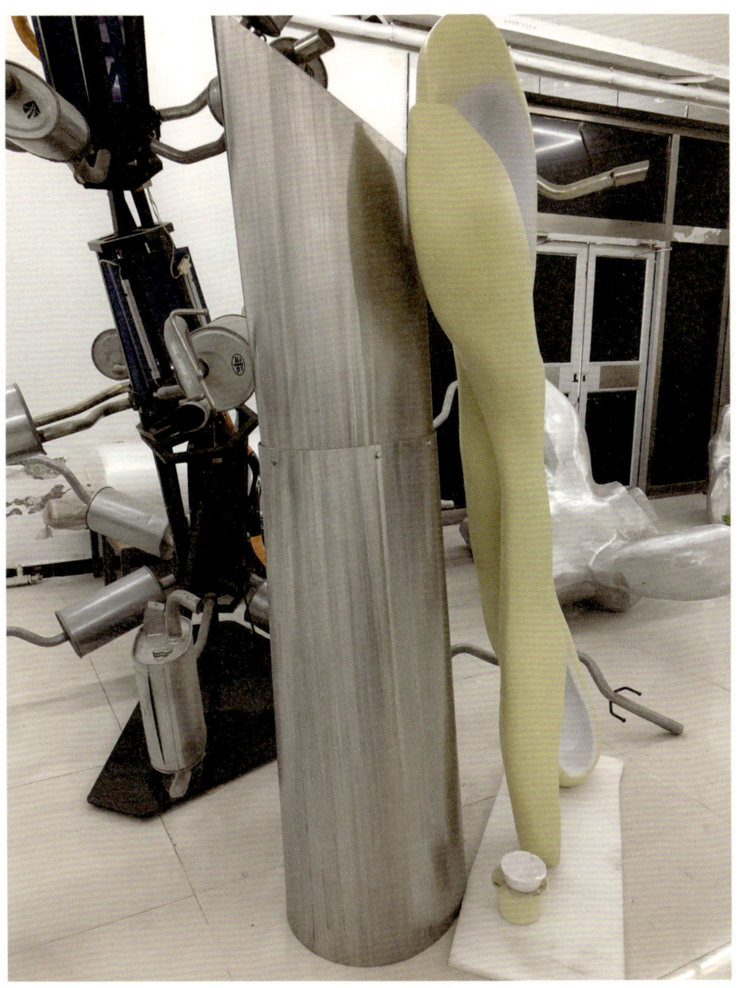

*Everything is possible. The implication is that there might be flaws and consequences for refusing to acknowledge the flaws i.e., doing as one pleases.*

## NOT EVERYTHING USED LEAVES A TRACE

When we say, ‘art is a sense of something unfinished’, we mean art is always larger than life at that moment, fundamentally refusing to revert to some knowledge or some equivalent reference object. For example, ‘like a mirror, it reflects…’. Even if it is comparable to a mirror, the mirror and the reflection can never be the same from different perspectives. An experience at a particular time is never the same as another, so we can’t, in the name of experiencing, experience on someone else’s behalf. For an atheist, the perspective of God cannot be replaced. I cannot speak for the work of art because, now that it has come into being, we are equal and it possesses more characteristics than I know. I am only sure about one thing – my work hinges on the fact that I can never exhaust its existence.

Actually, when I am more relaxed in my interpretation of my 'art studio', it allows for more freedom and I am no longer fixated on its distinctiveness, which arises as a result of restrictions to the interpretation of the world. For all things in the world, even before I see them, they have already been operating smoothly. From a biological perspective, humans and other species feed on each other. As a result, symbiosis becomes a hidden secret. Since I cannot photosynthesise, I can only feed on plants that can. Along with the plants, the bacteria that live quietly in the stems and fibres eagerly enter my body; they rush through my intestines, dying to be excreted so that they can feed on the delicacy – my stinky stool. Before they are excreted, my digestive functions, skin health and the operation of my internal organs largely depend on them – their density in my intestines may affect my nerves, make me feel pain or anxiety; at the same time, they may assist the normal function of my stomach and keep my head cool. Nevertheless, these minuscule bacteria have not revealed the full range of their functions to humans yet. I firmly believe that scientific progress always lags behind the evolution of bacteria and viruses, so much so that one could even say science trails behind bacteria. I could never know about a certain bacterium ahead of its development; I can only wait for it to take effect – only then would I realise why my stomach aches and bloats. My limited understanding of the bacterium that I have overlooked or even felt hostility towards illustrates how inadequate my knowledge is. It once again reminds me of the fact that bacteria, as an object, cannot be completely exhausted. Such a bacterial perspective keeps changing my perspective.

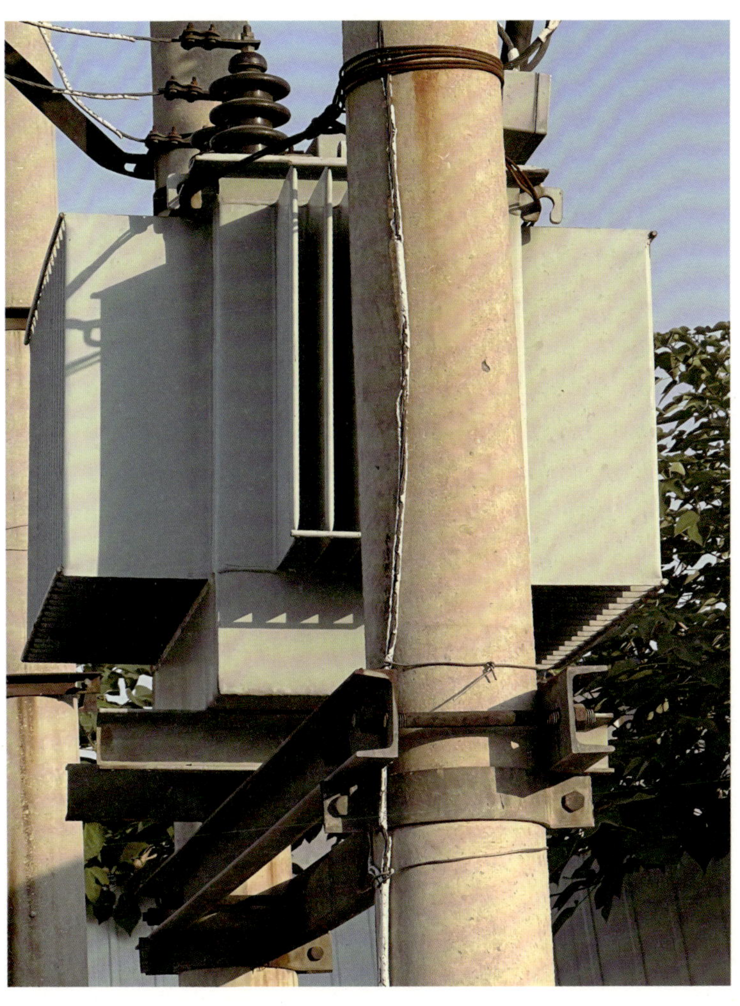

*The stable output of the transformer allows all the tools – the computer, the electric drill, the light bulb – to have an environment of their own. They are put to good use and have built an ecosystem around themselves, which also involves me, my assistant and other users of the tools. I must abide by the rules of the ecosystem of this setting. Beyond this ecosystem, on the other side of the door, there is a bigger ecosystem, all connected: restaurants are constantly bought and sold; there are more and more slogans on the walls, etc.*

## LARGER THAN THE PART 'USEFUL' TO ME

I only notice that the electric saw has cut off the wood bit by bit, but I am neither sure about the exact way it operates nor its next movement. I have no drawing, data or 'precise' steps. In most cases, I am at a point in between my imagination and the full capacity of the tools. I rely on my experiences, but how the electric saw, the wood and I interact is not subject to experiences – experiences can't generate enough solutions. Chance hangs in the air with no place to land – my brain, the tools or the wood. Even as time goes by, I would not know the exact landing point. Even if I can make partial deductions based on my past experiences, I cannot exhaust the possibilities of the present. This process has created the following fact: I make a decision for the electric saw to go forward and leftward for 5cm. However, I stop here, as it is not 'good' enough. Is it too straight or too deep? It is neither, but that's what I want. At 20cm from the gap, I cut forward and rightward for another 5cm. Alternatively, I may turn the wood over and repeat the last step. The difference is that such an action generates more frustration. As frustration accumulates, focus is generated as a byproduct.

In this process, I also only notice what I pay attention to. I have to admit, even if I can provide a long list, I cannot understand how chance lands on the surface of any object. The possibilities of a marvellous detail or an accidental occurrence of an arc cannot be exhausted no matter how we calculate from the perspectives of aesthetics, mathematics, engineering, biology or certain particularities of artists. Moreover, I cannot say that, beyond a certain consciousness, an unspeakable truth, there exists an incomprehensible 'thing in itself'. All I want to say is, this arc takes shape in an unexpected way and cannot be proved with any list. It is always larger than the part 'useful' to me.

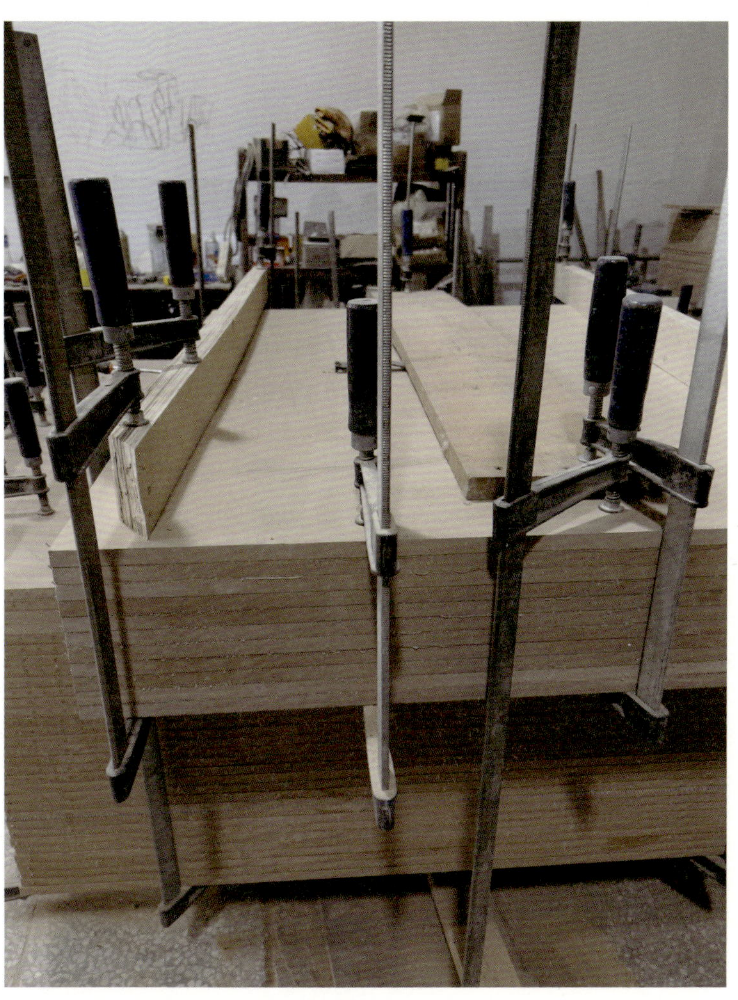

*Just like that, the user of an object (such as an F-clamp) will inevitably have a knowledge gap about it. My consciousness and experiences cannot fully explain this object. At the same time, the F-clamp does not behave unscrupulously just because I have extricated myself from a difficult situation and it has become my object of trial with my renewed freedom. The F-clamp is destined to ensure my work is just a specific piece of work. After I have done what is needed, and with a liberated approach, I will devote more time to the F-clamp and add specific meanings to my liberty.*

# CHAPTER 3

## THE CAUSE AND THE EFFECT OF DENSENESS

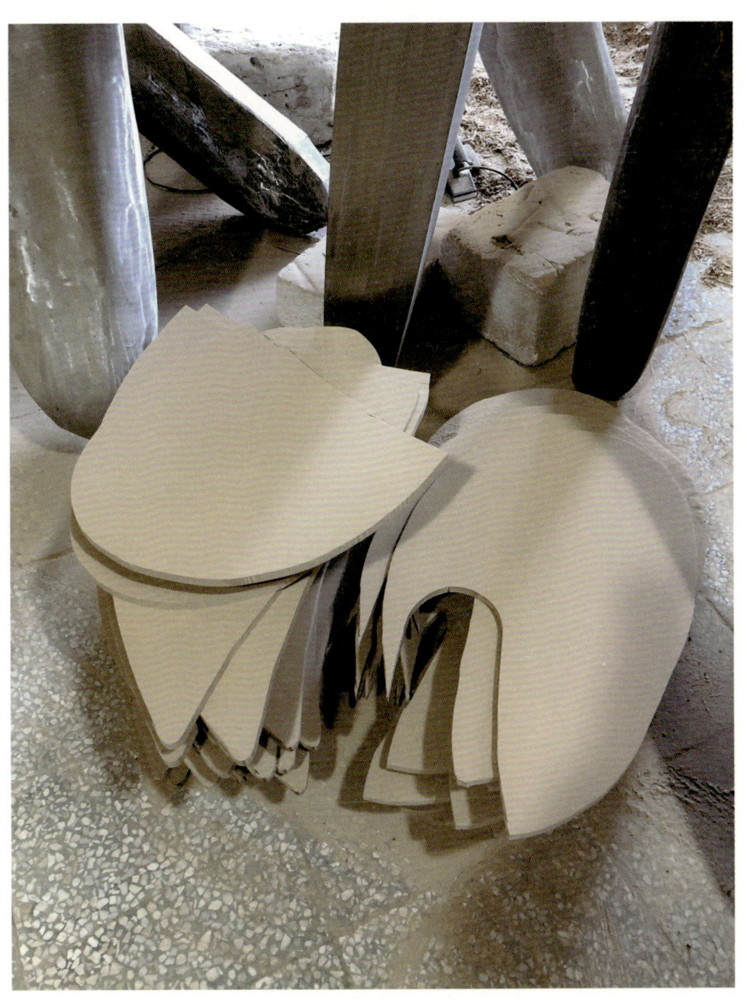

*They are not just 'materials' for art. Even though, through our interaction with them, we produce works of art eventually, they exist as a 'thing-in-itself' before art is created.*

## OSB

I use OSB in large quantities. Its raw materials are pieces of scrap wood, which are pulverised into tiny pieces, steam-compressed, moulded and then cut into pieces. Of course, the producers (factory workers) and users (construction workers) of OSB all use it in the usual way – for interior decoration, as materials for cupboards, doors and windows. Just because I use it differently, it does not need a new name to distinguish between its original function and its current one.

However, OSB means something different to me. I no longer have to limit myself to various types of wood – teak, ash, pine, and so on – as OSB has replaced all types of wood and has emerged as a new material. At the same time, I could say it is a type of environmentally friendly material. As such, this object has a whole new set of characteristics (energy-saving, clean, recyclable, sustainable, and so on).

Apart from the above-mentioned characteristics, OSB also fits my criteria for materials and things. Its colour is in between those of wood and clay – milder and more ambiguous. Yet, despite its soft-looking surface, it is hard, sturdy and sharp but also fragile and easily broken at the edges. Moreover, as it's made through compression, its density is higher than that of wood and therefore heavier than it seems. We have such detailed, even excessive, descriptions. For example, when we say it's a type of environmentally friendly material, we are speaking partially outside the scope of materials. However, I am still unable to pinpoint the position of OSB in the world of plentiful names that we give to things and, therefore, I am unable to establish its relationship with the rest of the world, as well as its meaning.

Based on the above description and thoughts, I cannot deduce my understanding of OSB to simply 'this is OSB!' Or even resort to a simpler approach – mark it out in the dictionary.

Because among all its known characteristics, I still cannot point out exactly which one makes it stand out.

As an aggregation of those characteristics, OSB has now become one of the materials I am using. They pile up in one corner of my studio, layer by layer, sheet by sheet, in an orderly manner that is aesthetic in itself. Afterwards, they are cut into pieces, into shapes. In a process of repeated cutting, their 'future' keeps getting modified. At the same time, the irregular, accidental pieces that are cut off become another view, occupying another spot in the studio, their continuity and haphazardness always flowing until they are recognised by others, including me, as 'a piece of work'. While it goes beyond the identity of OSB, it asks a question of itself: What is this? If not OSB, then what?

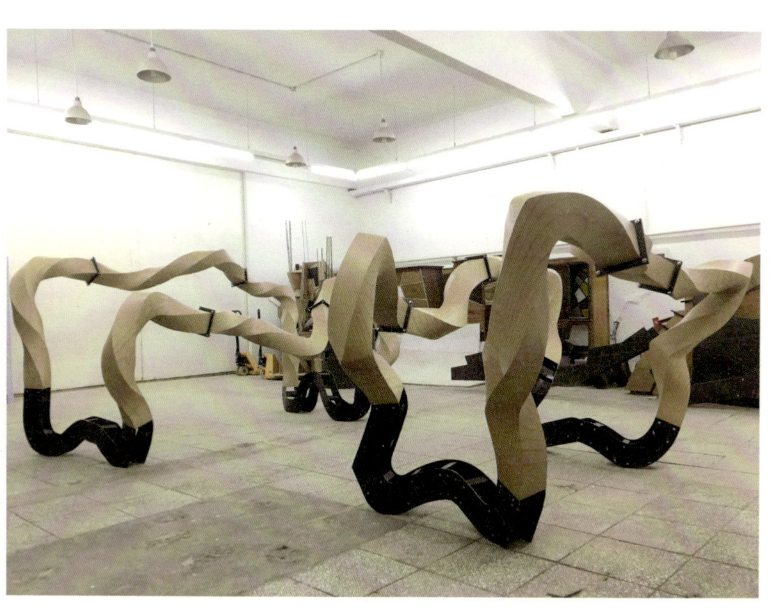

*No one knows exactly when this started, but there are clues everywhere. Because of the multitude of clues, the potential paths one could take have become much more diverse. As a result, there is more room for entanglement. To understand how such entanglement happens, one needs to understand what has caused it.*

## 'DRAFT'

The evolution of an object usually gets overwritten by the 'draft'. A 'draft' executes a certain order, just like a program, which diverts attention to execution. Though just a 'draft', it has somewhat dictated the future direction: a boundary has been quietly established – some sort of mechanical execution which is often mistaken for the artist's perception taking control of the object. A 'draft' does not allow for sensibility. What appears on the surface of a 'draft' – the emotions and openness to the future – slowly disappears over the course of execution, diverting attention to the certainty of a decision over 'the next step'. It also creates an illusion, as if every subsequent choice is a natural consequence. However, to elaborate, the 'choice' of the object itself is ignored. We'd rather treat it as dumb or blind and, instead, blindly follow the 'draft', which is based on human intention.

The 'draft' modifies the object and significantly limits its concreteness. The 'draft' slowly reduces the endless possibilities that the surface of the object initially possesses. Even though the artist always talks about possibilities, these disappear nightmarishly as if they are travelling along the perspectival lines to a fixed vanishing point; they are just dice to be rolled to bet on the future. Only then would we discover the evil of the 'draft'. It was its value that inspired the artist to create it in the first place; initially, it seemed to be very open about the future, but its face quickly turned ferocious. However, just like the evolutionary processes of all living things, there are always the 'chosen' survivors.

Actually, a 'draft' is only a product of symbiosis – we should respectfully accept this fact. A new piece of work is created, not just from the artist's all-encompassing imagination, but also the collective that supports such imagination. Even at the very beginning, numerous surrounding factors supported and nourished this imagination; unlike what we human beings describe – merely a bunch of mindless symbols or abstract concepts – drafts participate in the so-called action of the artist's imagination. We do not notice them because we are making use of them. This is not a discussion on ethics, but merely a fact. As far as imagination is concerned, the artist is not to be put on a pedestal.

First of all, this collective imagination includes perceptions that are not exclusive to human beings but the result of a billion years of evolution for all organisms. Every tree around us, every stone and every stick insect crawling on the studio floor has such perceptions. Moreover, I, along with all the perceptive organisms and plants, am constantly changing; no single force may decisively control how other things change. Perceivers have different levels of perceptiveness – some more powerful than others. Such differences in degree allow for so-called diversity, which helps to maintain an equality of everything in our symbiotic environment.

So-called chance, therefore, is not something that can be explained by words alone. Chance acts as the mask of complexity while continually maintaining its 'stability' – it only appears when and where it is needed. In addition, chance doesn't just stay in one place at a point in time, waiting for our capture: chance flows like air in our every action and process. Finally, the chance that we imagined isn't that powerful; it is fragile because, unlike human organs that are protected by lymph nodes or human immunity that can be protected against viruses through vaccination, chance doesn't have protection or immunity. Yet, 'others' can still break our limited immunity, causing us to constantly get infected. As such, we and 'others' achieve symbiosis through infection.

There is a possibility that human ancestors, eucalyptus trees and fungi share the same origin, as biologist Lynn Margulis' theory indicates. Therefore, this might be a world that originated from the same bacterium three billion years ago. As the bacterium were free to wander around, they developed symbiotic relationships, entered into one another and, enabled by DNA, effectuated the evolution of cells through symbiotic mergers. That is one theory of how human beings came about. This is not just a biological concept. Symbiosis happens among many other things: a family protected by law, a traditional proverb, a lesson from art history, an artist and his work… all are part of symbiotic relationships. Still more new members are joining – new bacterium and their family and friends.

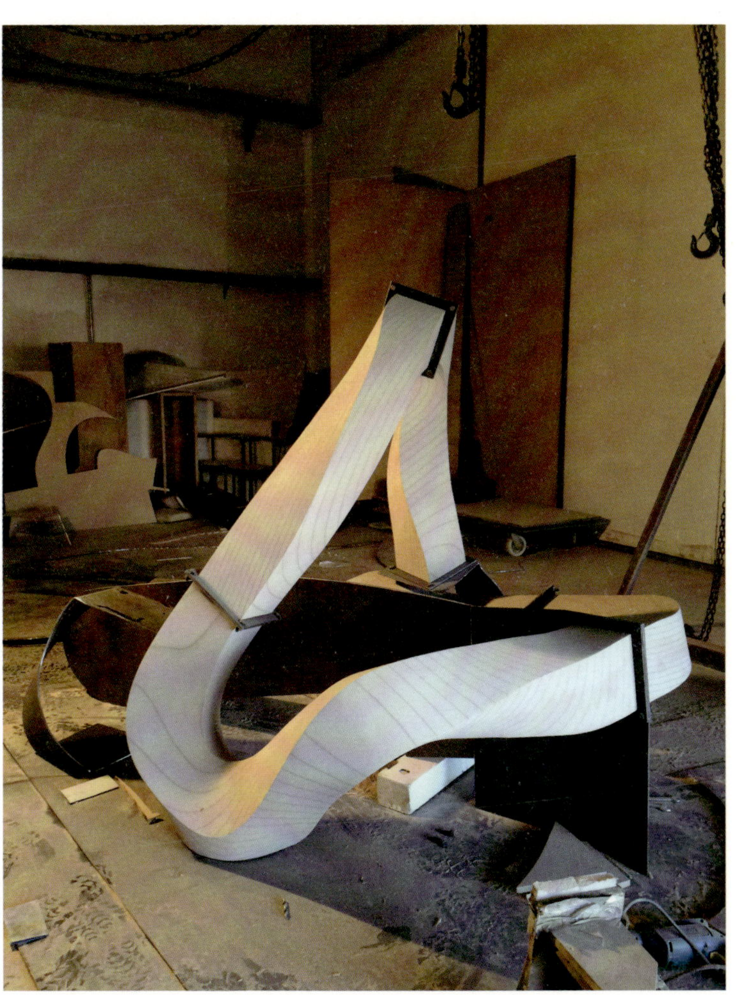

*One apparent source of power comes from a countering force – one that goes against our 'going with the flow'. Such power is beyond our control. Interestingly, even though strange to us, it impacts us strongly. Today, such influences mostly come from nonhumans.*

In today's world, nonhumans are undoubtedly part of our family, as our lives become closely related to theirs. Though they are sometimes thought to be invaders, they are in fact painstakingly taking care of us. Starting each morning, when we switch on the computer or our mobile phone, we obtain feeds for our brain; we take various forms of transportation to go from one place to another. Whether we like it or not, our bodies are protecting us the same way we protect them, no matter how we interpret protection.

Such symbiosis created 'us' from me and them. 'We' become an item. My relationship with 'us' keeps evolving: I use tools to pass my genes to 'us'; 'our' body opens up to me and we don't just exchange information but also create impact on one another. Without symbiosis, an object is just a material or a collection of its characteristics, minus the defining details of the object itself. I apply skills to make changes to these characteristics; changes prove that my work is the result of symbiotic evolution of me and my materials.

Imagine this scene: at the beginning, I just want to use a 'draft' to initiate an action. In fact, at this point, many participants are ready to take action: the wood, the tools, the power supply, the aluminium alloy, the emulsion glue and myself. All of us have been mobilised, not to act upon the directions given by the 'draft', but to vault over our own limits and show the fluid relationships among things. The wooden board allows the curved saw to cut through its body, the two acting like a surfboard and waves – the surfboard keeps sailing forward smoothly through wave after wave; the waves bring with them energies that both push the board forward and compel the surfer to react accordingly in order to balance. In this way, symbiosis creates equality: to ride along the waves, always mustering all participants to discreetly balance one with the other and allowing us to live in a world of equality among all things. If we miss any single participant, we will hit a deadlock; any arbitrary, unilateral delay will trigger the failure of the entire action. Maybe that is the secret behind the fact that art today necessarily entails symbiosis.

No instrument can capture the traces of these secrets for they have no technical indicators, no vector analysis, not even any justifiable volume. Their existence does not rely on our consciousness; they occasionally catch our attention and gently smile at the observer, in the same way that we encounter moments in nature: wind blows on water, making new objects in the process – ripples and waves.

There is no such thing as sculpture materials. In the process of sculpting, they would gradually lose their material aspect and integrate into the new creation, blending into the new environment and losing their characteristics as pure materials. In symbiosis, each participant more or less loses part of its past. In this process, the limits of a straight saw sabotage the completeness of the 'draft'. Heat injects dryness into the body of the wood. I am 'betrayed' by the confidence I had yesterday. All of these share a new common background and are clashing, arguing, fighting with and enduring one another. As time passes by, part of this process becomes understood and is taken away, part of it disappears and only some leave traces. Any tracing back only has literal meaning. We are left with something blurry, not enough to be the proof of some concrete result. Maybe this is another way of interpreting art.

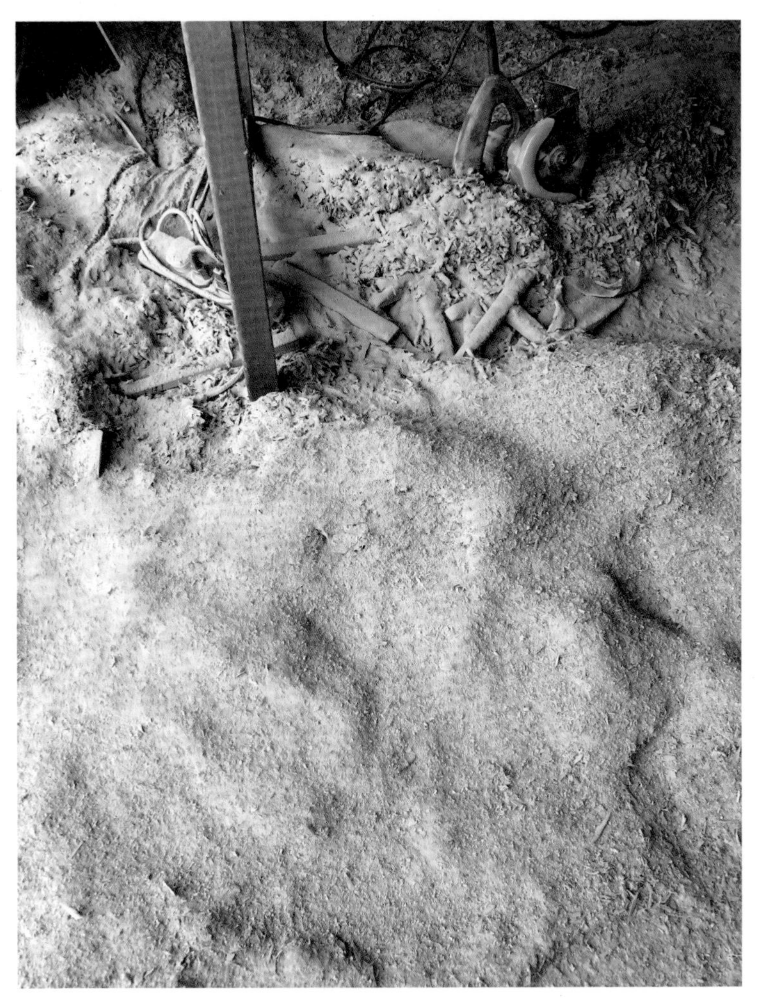

*It could be counted as a form of belief which, just like keeping fit, requires regular exercise.*

# NORMAL CHOICE

Being bland yet experiencing plenty of twists and turns – these two apparent extremes always happen at the same time. On one hand, I hope to maintain a 'normal', 'external' working environment at the studio – no power or water outage, no last-minute demolition and relocation notice, no accidents as far as possible, and so on. Such external conditions have become a norm and directly affect how the studio operates. On the other hand, such uncontrollable events are often on my mind in my daily life – avoiding accidents has come into such sharp focus and 'no accident' seems so bland, with total predictability and dullness. Two things are true almost at the same time. In fact, there is no way for me to make a clear decision and all decisions stem from the allocation of choices. When I escape from the singular me, I stand among the plural form of me. I become part of the things; I have lost my special right to choose – I am merely placed among things to be chosen. This is a universal choice or a normal choice, without the limitations and hurdles of a 'conscious choice'. A normal choice grants fairness to all things. Such fairness exists because we have lost our unilateral power of choosing among things, which comes about almost always when we make 'conscious choices'.

Based on my understanding, the creation of a painting is the result of such a 'normal choice'. From the images in each frame of a 5-minute-long video clip to all things captured on a 2m-by-2m blank canvas, no single item is the result of a 'conscious choice', and this leads to a new future. First of all, they are no longer constrained by the 'conscious choice' or bound by categories based on meanings, symbols, analogies, implications; they can appear in any order without any prior indication. Such an order is controlled by a technique more complex than I can grasp. I cannot pretend to showcase an image created by the new technique and I have to admit that I have lost the ability to produce the images and investigate their sources. In a symbiotic relationship with my mobile phone and my computer, I turn into the plural form of myself – to decide or be decided, to support or negate. As such, on a new vessel – the blank canvas – the half forms and the plural forms confront one another, the background and the images repeatedly alternate and rapidly change: human skin tone, race, gender and posture disappear in plants' stems and stalks or mountains' surfaces and cross-sections. An image skips a frame, or the computation of a number stumbles on screen, a video image of the asexual and boring underwater world from 370 million years ago in the Devonian Period is played, tubers sprout from underground and photosynthesise for the first time.... Such images are neither created by the artist, nor are they the result of the artist's 'conscious choices'. Whether a flash of inspiration or vanishing into thin air, they do not just happen in a specific space, as an incident or a consequence of a certain logic, or as a new organism, a new human race or a new species. Instead, they are the result of a 'normal choice', a flat result.

In this world of 'normal choices', my remaining parts and I live in a symbiotic environment with fire extinguishers, cats, fossils of the Ediacaran rock, rhinos, elephants, fluorocarbon paint, turpentine and everything else. It is not my doing but simply my being in this environment.

An art studio usually has clear boundaries, not just in terms of space but, more importantly, perception. The studio is where the artist showcases his ability and, to a large extent, where the artist is expected to work. It is a fixed production site for the artist. On one hand, it is surrounded by backdrops and various physical conditions – walls that are high enough, spaces with movable frames, multifarious tools placed accordingly and tabletops for sculpture-making. On the other hand, these conditions form the landscape of the artist's work environment, bringing the artist into his phenomenological scene of self, allowing him to work in a self-consistent environment (including designs that are self-consistent). The work takes place in a natural environment which minimises the chance of strangers trespassing – not only on the level of consciousness but also the actual probabilities of seeing new things. A 'surprising' space is cut down to form a static scene of the art studio.

The appearance of these tangible items set the scene at the studio. However, whenever an action takes place, the internal parts of the tangible items keep breaking down, separating and reorganising, so as to give birth to new objects and a new 'environment'. When the weather is cold, insufficient heating results in bodily stiffness and lethargy, which in turn affects the action of the artist when he carries out his work on the objects. The original postures that the artist struck in order to focus on his work are changed and the gestures become unnatural: the way he deploys the pen, the knife and the polisher are different from his muscle memories, hence the occurrence of dislocations and imbalance. Hot weather leads to lack of blood supply to the brain and delayed vision. 'Normal choices' appropriately embrace such chance incidents that are otherwise excluded, allowing us to accept more honestly how limited our impact on the environment is.

A 'normal choice' is a process that slows down to allow more interaction between humans and nonhumans. As a result, I view a series of numbers with alternative perspectives – they always come unexpectedly. We could also say that a 'specific choice' stems from distrust – the need to categorise – which eventually results in fear of the unknown. Even if we accept these 'guests', we are temporarily isolating them outside our trust and brush them off with ethics, as we remain extremely vigilant to strangers.

However, up to now, these ‘guests’ that we guard against have no intention of harming anyone.

All indecisiveness comes from distrust – a ‘normal choice’ is a way to get rid of such self-fear through collective actions.

# CHAPTER 4

## SWALLOW AND DISCHARGE

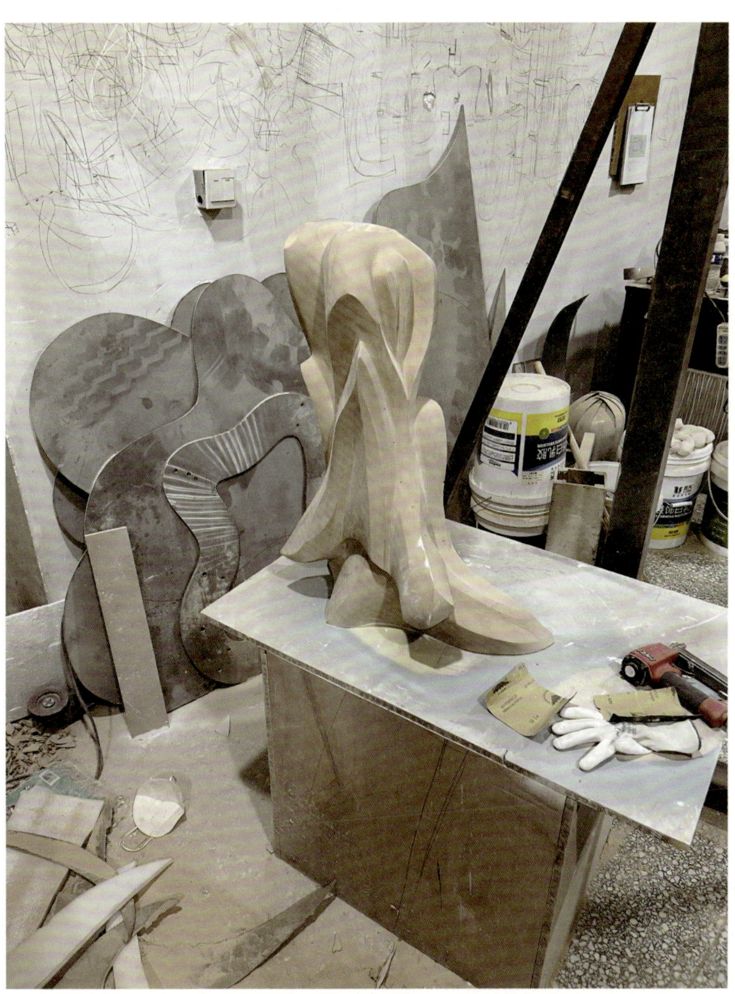

*No matter how I focus on changing my mindset with total devotion, I am still not 'in front of' the object.*

# ALL ARE INGREDIENTS

Flowering plants attract butterflies and bees to pollinate for them, reproducing in places further afield through these insects' help.

Manmade objects inherit DNA, formed as a result of symbiosis among humans and plants. In the world of biology, such a common case of 'mutual influence' isn't a secret. A building is like a flowering plant: its giant torso, dazzling façade and ever-changing geometric shapes are all features to attract attention from numerous animals – human beings who can move with legs – to accomplish the mission of spreading the word. As such, architecture seduces its 'owner' – creator, architect – to be its 'servant' and voluntarily spread the word for it. People willingly come to the building, take photos of it with various tools, mobilise their sensory organs to present the building's various parts as standalone images, which are then carried through different forms of media and spread to the world just like seeds.

Like buildings, gallery and museum exhibits – paintings, sculptures, installations and video projected and repeatedly played on a screen hanging on the wall – are manmade objects, though much smaller in scale. Their lineage can also be traced back to the symbiosis among humans and other organisms; they are proof of the perfect marriage between the propagation of plants and the mobility of animals over millions of years of evolution. In exhibition halls, artworks inherit the wisdom of flowering plants and wait patiently for their loyal pollinators: paintings that are full of attractive colours and enchanting vibes, as well as large installations and sculptures that attract attention with their complex shapes and volumes, though lack the muscle and nervous system of animals hence their remaining fixed like plants. Those two-legged animals – visitors – arrive, 'devour' the artworks with their consciousness and sensory organs and carry them around in their bodies to eventually discharge them at various places in various ways. Perhaps just at the roadside, after a cup of coffee, they are dumped into the urban sewage system. Some of them are carried to various conferences and seminars where, through language and sound, they are spread to more strangers, who carry these fruits to even more places further afield. Some other 'lucky' ones are recorded on paper to become the next 'fruits' to be 'devoured'.

The devourers and the dischargers are creating a new metaphor, which quietly substitutes the realities that have disappeared from paintings, sculptures and installations, allowing the attractiveness and forms to remain on the wall and the ground. The devourers use their senses to absorb parts of the artworks and then bring them along. A play of symbiosis is continually performed, embodying the secret of artistic metaphor.

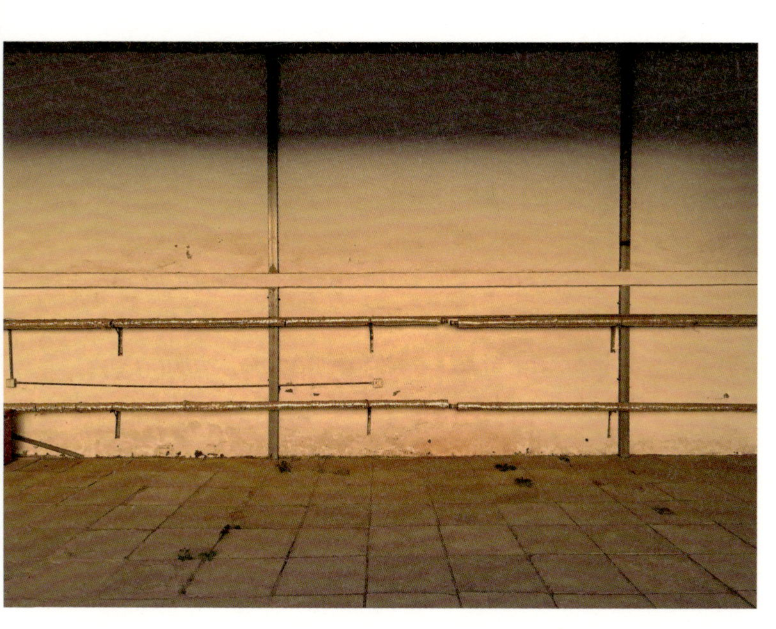

*I am either already contained in something (the room, the light, the table, and so on) or in the process of becoming part of something (the weather, the birds and the people walking by the gate).*

# THOSE WITH SHELLS

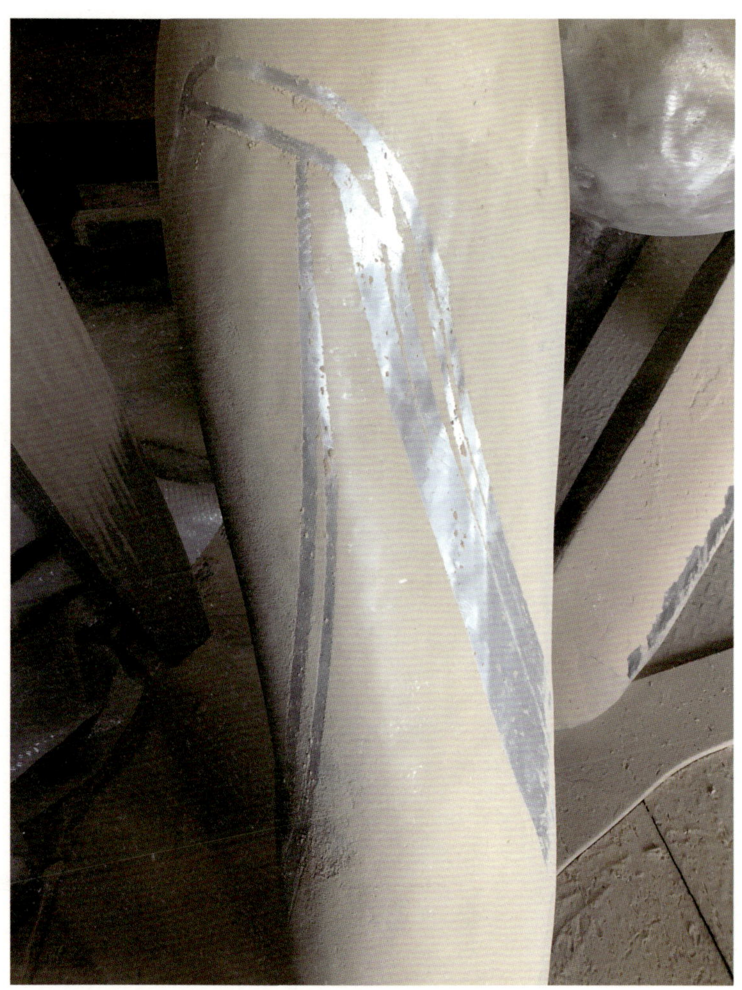

*We must resist the conclusions already known to us, including the knowledge that is camouflaged as feelings.*

For food with shells, such as peanuts and walnuts, as well as those with skins, such as oranges and watermelons, we always directly remove these shells and skins in order to enjoy the delicious content. Human beings are not alone in doing this. When monkeys take bananas from zookeepers, they, too, peel the skins and only swallow the fragrant, sweet fruit inside. Some anthropologists even use bananas as an analogy for Asians – yellow skin on the outside and illusions of being white on the inside. Such characteristics of things have inspired the imagination of phenomenology. It was Edmund Husserl who first brought to our attention the distinction between appearance and content.

Things with shells test our ability to focus. The shell exists to protect the core, and the core is always surrounded by the shell. Therefore, by neglecting and discarding the shell, we are making a sacrifice. To philosophers, shells are solid surfaces that always arouse feelings in us with their attractive appearances, making us linger between the object's and our own sensations. Just like the coffee is hidden under the foam, nothing reveals its function if you only look at the appearance. This has nothing to do with mysticism, but is an intensification of our being. For everything – a building, a painting, a sculpture, a bridge – the appearance and the substance hidden underneath exist in such a cruel, cold-blooded way. Could art survive and retreat from there?

To a large extent, we might only be dealing with shells and not the content inside. Graham Harman distinguished between sensual qualities and real qualities: we will only appreciate qualities that we can sense. The reality retreats, thereby giving significance to metaphor.

When an artist imagines something, the metaphor is already implied. On one hand, this metaphor points to the superficial that we could sense and the hidden substance that we could not reach. On the other hand, no matter how we plan ahead and fully use our imagination, narrate and conclude afterwards, we are unable to reach the essence of what was indirectly represented by the metaphor.

Art must create a way to 'replace'. Things that upset us can no longer be explained by words or hijacked by diagrams but only felt by whoever comes to appreciate it.

Conceptualism emphasises a potential risk-free way of working, which is essentially surrendering to the shell. The inability to distinguish between appearance and substance results in an overload of knowledge for people and things. Consequently, we lose the opportunity to get one step closer to the substance. Precisely at this step, we distance ourselves from the things and from the reality.

We are only processing things as we understand them rather than concentrating on what they actually are. How many words and forms of media do we have to get through to reach that piece of iron sheet lying on the ground in empty space? This is not trying to prove flat ontology; this is about the iron sheet turning into an object in our consciousness.

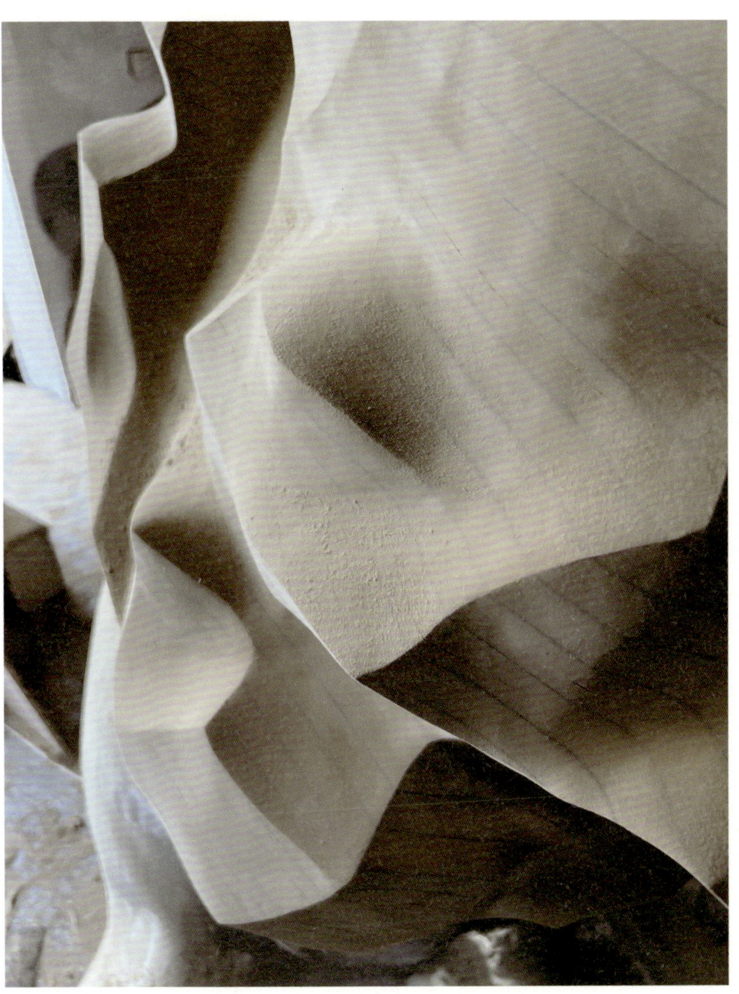

*Dust particles settle on the wood, simultaneously preventing me from seeing properly and covering up the surface of the wood. As I resort to continually sweeping off the dust, it is gone, along with its chance to create a new surface for the wood. The wood remains.*

# WHAT IS DISTURBING ME, MAKING ME RESTLESS

Those fish lie side by side on the ice cubes. I can somewhat recognise some of them for their delicious taste; others make a lasting impression because of their sheer quantity, the space that they take up. I pause, as my eyes suddenly catch a flash of bright red. On top of the pile at one stall, that strip of red is specially dazzling. It is a red fish, similar in length and looks to the rest – even the way it is lying is the same as the rest. The only difference is its skin colour. I am attracted to its appearance and temporarily forget that it's a fish, i.e., that it can be eaten.

Perhaps in half an hour or an hour, a chef will come here and take it away. Later this evening, it will appear on a dining table somewhere in this city, but it won't be alone as it will come with soup and seasoning; it will no longer be itself, no longer as bright. As its attractive appearance disappears, it becomes food.

To David Hume, things don't exist, only their characteristics. When we encounter characteristics such as red, succulent and sweet, that thing is then an apple. Husserl saw a flaw in Hume's logic, however, and told us that the characteristics of a thing cannot determine the thing itself. He made a distinction between characteristics and content. Phenomenology insists that, be it characteristic or content, only when it appears in our consciousness, does it have value. Phenomenology does not acknowledge things outside our consciousness. According to this line of thought, I only need to focus on the dash of red and not bother with the disappearance of the fish as food behind the redness.

According to Martin Heidegger, we do not directly interact with things; on the contrary, only when they run into 'problems', do we realise that these things have been working for us all the time. In his famous example, he wrote about a covered railway platform. The platform is not merely a summation of physical materials; when it rains, we vaguely develop the idea of not wanting to get wet. Thus, the platform disappears from our consciousness, becoming part of the background; 'taking shelter from the rain' becomes an image and creates a new space.

In my case, it's the colour – red. Whether I notice the colour or not, the fish is there. The same fish could appear at different places in different people's consciousness – to a chef, it represents something delicious; to a seller, it is just a commodity. We can further imagine that days before it is laid on the ice cubes, it was swimming in the east ocean before being caught by a fisherman. No matter what, we would not imagine that the chef is cooking a crab or that we are bargaining with the seller over a chicken. It is still a fish – it is the same object, though it is looked upon by different observers and users, at different times and in different ways that only relate to our perceptions.

Up to now, that fish is just an object of perception and only appears in my consciousness. Whether it is braised with soy sauce, whether I am attracted to its bright red, I cannot conclude that this is the fish. The real fish is more or less than our knowledge of it; whether I feel anything about it or completely ignore it, it is a real object that exists. This is the characteristic highlighted to us in object-oriented ontology by Harman.

# CHAPTER 5

## DEEP IN TIME

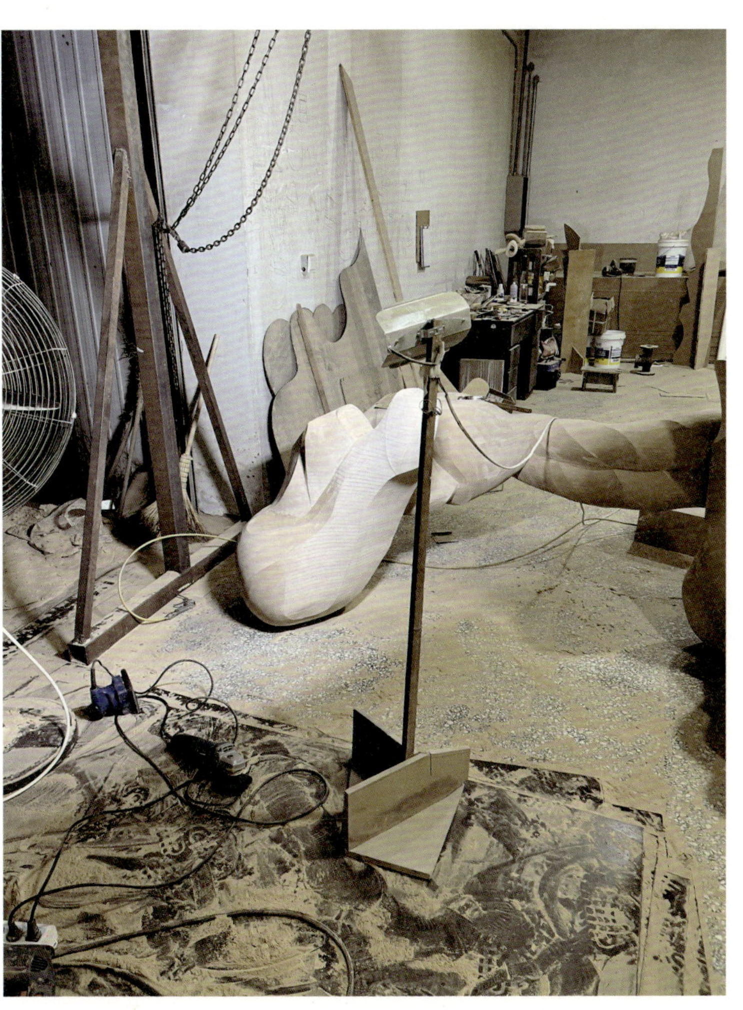

*Shaped like a little dragon, this object is laid on the floor. Every time it encounters other tools, its shape changes. It is sometimes straight (for a few days in a row), sometimes bent (for another few days) and sometimes twisted (for even longer). However, I never mistake it for something else. It is constantly changing, moving and pausing every now and then. As it moves and pauses, time lapses.*

## ANCESTOR

An organism with neither head nor tail was discovered in 1965 in Philadelphia, on the wall of a marine-life pond. At the time of the discovery, it was slowly crawling around. It is proven to be one of the smallest organisms – a trichoplax. As Lynn Margulis put it, having neither head nor hind end, right nor left side, no eyes, no stomach, this minuscule slow crawler gives away the secret of its animality only at reproduction. Did it come from the Cambrian Period 500 million years ago? Or maybe even earlier, before numerous life forms emerged? It is difficult to imagine if the cleaner that made the discovery realised that it was perhaps our ancestor. How did this little organism in the pond sense its surroundings and us, its descendants – those animals that were wearing sunglasses, chewing gum, holding their mobile phones and taking photos of the animals swimming didn't even acknowledge its presence. No matter what, it was indeed a life living in the same ecosystem as us and its appearance was like a piece of jigsaw puzzle previously missing to complete the big picture of our history of evolution. First of all, this organism gives us the opportunity to understand our present from a much longer-term perspective. This life form came way before the first human being was able to stand on their feet. It had no eyes but had most likely understood the history of mankind as we told ourselves. Residing on the wall of the pond, it 'witnessed' the human bodies that survived the aftermath of European Wars and the Pacific War and came with prostheses; it 'heard about' 'Resist US And Help North Korea', the dictatorship of the proletariat, the October Revolution and Mai 68 – all the historical events that made us lament with fear and disgust. Of course, we have memories that extend beyond these events – the mysterious Sanxingdui masks; the secrets behind the Qin army's forging of weapons, many of which were left in numerous caves; the massive collections of images also hidden in the caves – all of which belong to the past of human beings. The slimy existence of the trichoplax, however, allows us to appreciate an era before human history, helping us to rise above our narrow perspective over the shallow past of our own kind.

To turn time into history is still a form of governance by human being.

We often see a familiar diagram of the evolution of man: from a hairy animal walking on all fours, then slowly shedding the long hair, to gradually standing and walking on two feet. As we shed the hair, our smooth skin became the intermediary between our body and the outside world, hence it required protection. As a result, we killed the apes that did not evolve into human beings, along other hairy animals, and used their fur as clothing. The evolution of any species would involve some degree of cruelty, but only we humans have the ability to narrate such evolutions. Therefore, we crafted our history of evolution in a perfect and detailed way to cover up the violence we used to make up for our deficiencies. Darwin called this process 'natural selection'.

Through diagrams, footnotes and records, we try to appreciate the ascent of human beings. We constantly live in this illusion of nobility until, one day, when I was running with my dog alongside the river and being dragged along, unable to catch up, he turned his head over as if to tell me: four legs are faster than two.

Remains of arguably the earliest human art were found on the rocks of Grotte de Lascaux in France. These art pieces or paintings were simple in form, yet difficult to decipher. Only four-legged animals such as antelopes, cows and deer are depicted; two-legged beings are nowhere to be seen. According to art history textbooks, this is a demonstration of our love for nature and also the starting point of drawing, this very human technique. However, if the animals in the drawings could speak, you might hear a different voice: envy us? Turn back. Four legs are better because, aesthetically, four contact points are stabler, more metaphysical and more artistic.

Are those so-called 'aesthetically valuable' images definitely created with love? Perhaps they were merely to mark down a delicious meal – a note on biological evolution or simply a list of food? After all, for 'hunters' to consume a species much bigger in size and quantity than themselves, it must have meant serious challenges to their capabilities – they had to pay the price and put in the effort so as to survive. Let's reconsider what actually happened in Grotte de Lascaux from a biological point of view.

In a dark cave, a fire was lit, casting the hunters' shadows on the rocks. They were discussing a major hunt for the next day. The explorer briefed everyone on what he had seen – the animals that were destined to be eaten – but he was unsure if the prey would simply yield to their fate. Therefore, he randomly picked a stone from the ground, perhaps more pointed and harder than other stones. With the help of the fire, he found a rock with a relatively flat surface and drew out what he had seen earlier that day. He tried his best to make his drawing clear. When he used the stone to draw on the rock, he came up with those symbols. His body started to remember and recognise the symbols. Over time, the stone would evolve into a type of tool and the rock become the very first screen.

Today, screens have become a platform for the world. That particular stone was discarded long ago. With anaerobic bacteria crawling all over, this human tool decomposed and became a part of nature. At the same time, in much greater quantity, the microorganisms that had been living in the mud since the Cambrian Period survived negative oxygen and evolved over the course of a hundred million years. Quietly appearing from the depths of time, they simultaneously made up and acted upon time. Take silicon as an example. Silicon is not just a replacement of the stone; it controls the functioning of screens and reigns over new technology. When a chip is implanted, does the screen swallow the silicon, making silicon part of itself? Or does silicon devour the screen, making the screen its new face? Regardless, silicon orchestrated the new revolution of the world; it's everywhere – everything is such a plague and we, as a result, have become a foreign body to ourselves.

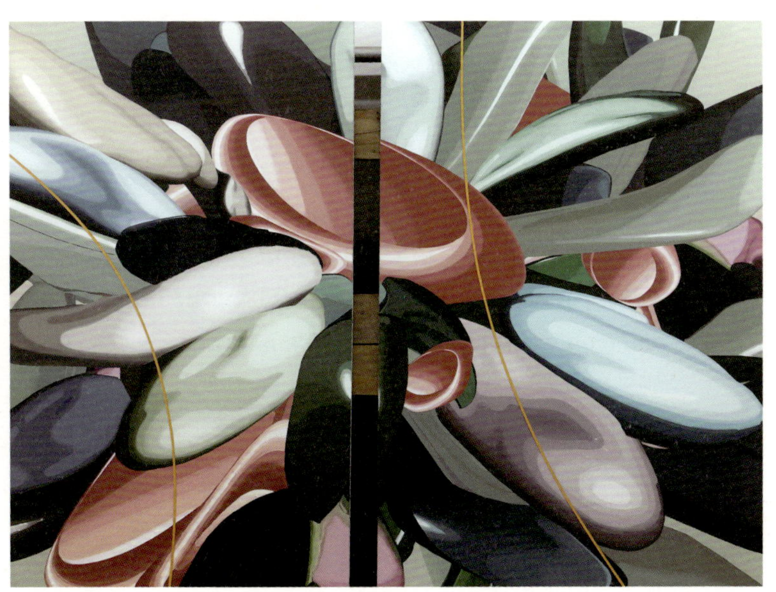

*If the world is truly equal, then, as I draw, my hand, the brush, the paint and the canvas will form a 'network of helpers', all of them participating in the making of the network.*

# FLAT

It's not necessarily true that the intention to create art around a certain object means that the process of using that object can be taken as the process of artmaking. Take a hoe as an example. When its usage and purpose is altered, it is allowed to vault over the limitations of its properties: it can still be used to hoe the field, remove weeds, loosen the soil, releasing more energy and giving the soil more potential, yet, formed by connecting a piece of cast metal and a piece of hard wood, it can also be displayed on a marble exhibition table, or fixed on an empty wall, or even attached to other materials to generate a new form of media. This is not to say that such a change results from the artist's illusory Midas touch but to describe the changing process of an object, its way of changing and the final product. Art is just one way of its being.

I only want to say, whether it's a tool for a farmer or a form of media used by an artist, the way it is produced isn't changed but it is given more associations. I am not claiming that users from different backgrounds automatically imbue the object with greater meaning (sociologically or politically). Moreover, according to the logic of traditional critical theory, it can further be used as some form of 'proof', to show that behind any single object there is a hidden manipulator.

The interaction between the artist and the hoe is no different from any other form of interaction. The hoe can be used on the soil, on the crops and sometimes even turned into a cold-blooded weapon to kill someone. Yet, the hoe can also be deconstructed by the artist and used on something else. As a result, the hoe interacts with the electric saw and the paint. All forms of interaction have the same limitation; all become equal. Such 'flatness' (in the sense of flat ontology) does not belittle the artist or reduce human knowledge.

We should accept the true equality that arises from such interaction. Precisely because artists don't fully understand the power and the limitation of their own actions, they are constantly in stand-offs with the objects that they work on. Such stand-offs are based on equality.

## TOO MUCH OR TOO LITTLE

I cannot calculate 'quantity'. Unlike sculptures, which come with fixed structures and confine the viewer's perspectives to the structures themselves, installations increasingly become trapped in the operation: all elements that appear at the site and make up the installation are damaged to varying degrees by the conceptualised organisation of all, hence losing their individuality as a form of media. Such individuality forms the basis of an object's being. That is to say, even when married with other things, an object's substance cannot be replaced, thereby reducing the chance of external manipulation.

To a large extent, this task is carried out in universality as I interact with all elements: a piece of cloth, colours, a piece of wood, a saw. On one hand, they present themselves to me in a beauty parade with their own distinct features that capture my attention; on the other hand, they disappear from the surface relationships, coincidentally and collectively escaping the limitations of the literal meanings attached to them, rendering them forever incomplete.

Only when they are used 'abnormally', do they reveal the functions that have been otherwise hidden in normal usage. Every fault leads to a new beginning. For example, I bought an electric drill specifically designed for drilling rocks. A lack of a certain metal component led to increasing breakages. However, when I overlooked this unresolvable defect and attempted to use it with a new object – wood – the drill unlocked functions not listed on the user manual. Its mission was changed and it became a sharper and more effective tool. It seems that the normality of product development, manufacturing and assembly processes led to the ineffectiveness of the design. So only when it was used abnormally, would it become normal. Such abnormality set it free from the original system and allowed it to become my new tool and partner.

## STAGGERING ALONG

Decisions made in 'a short time' or as emergency responses that are not 'well-thought-out' hold the secret to biological evolution. It is neither passive waiting nor intentional act. No single act is carried out entirely as it is intended from the beginning. Therefore, the initial work of the artist, to a certain extent, is not about art but about how to deal with materials. Materials come before art; they generate the initial work for the artist and allow him to be effective in his work. The fact that the ideas of the artist come before the materials makes his job unique. Such uniqueness is larger than art itself. Therefore, to disregard the original concept of 'materials' is perhaps the first step of the artist's work. This step turns the concept of materials into the object at hand, 'flattening' out the artist's work, whereby it is no longer able to use the 'perfect strategy' and be 'well-thought-out'. Haste is one of the techniques that artists could use to deal with the future – not to make art out of 'meaningful materials' but to fully open themselves up to the object and accept each and every encounter that the environment brings.

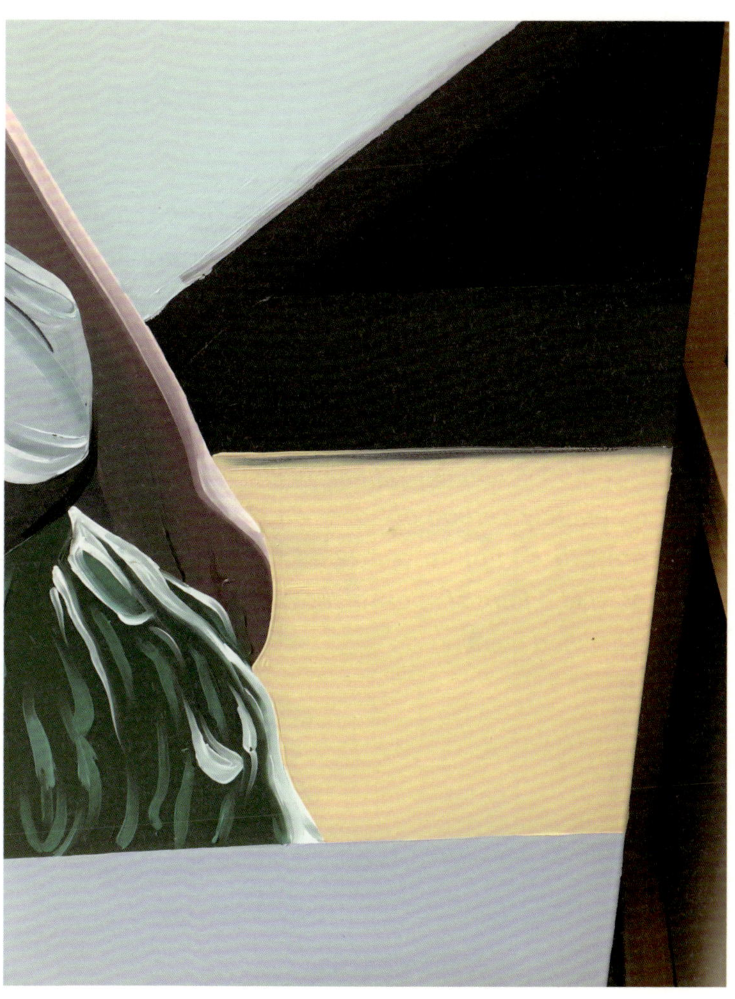

*Energy is released through the interaction between various objects. My hand holds a nylon-tip pen and draws out clear lines; when a weasel-hair paintbrush, with the tip shaped like a hazelnut, turns on the paper, it leaves a circular mark; paint requires the dilution of oil to travel on a canvas. These actions need to be repeatedly carried out over an ever-expanding area to complete a process. Yet, they only provide a form of release; they do not guarantee a finished painting.*

# CHAPTER 6

## ONCE SEEN, THEN IT'S NOT JUST ME

## MACHINE-GUIDED

To philosopher Marshall McLuhan, media is deeper than content. It is not just the provider and propagator of content, it can also interact with other media, giving rise to new means of expression. Broadly speaking, media is an extension of our senses as well as all objects that we interact with. At the same time, certain techniques enable faster work, supplementing the media used in the environment where the images are produced. Such compensation or supplementation makes us pay more attention to not just the tangible but also the environment and conditions which give rise to the tangible.

In the past, whenever I pointed the camera at an object, I would lose the depth of field. It wasn't the blur that resulted from the loss of focus that was the problem, but the objects that had disappeared in the flat background. If you give over control to the camera lens, then you will find only objects and not shapes in your viewfinder.

When I first went to a teahouse in Sichuan with my video camera, the whole teahouse seemed like a background: people, chairs and tables all seemed to be glued together in the same scene. My video camera and I, alongside farmers' baskets, carrying poles, tables, chairs, teacups, teapots, all co-existed in this environment. Only when I slowly moved my video camera along, were the people on the screen gradually 'separated' from the rest of the scene – they became speakers and listeners, a man, a middle-aged woman, a person wearing glasses, a person standing one metre away from the speaker. At the same time, apart from these people, a dog jumped out at a distance of three metres away, circling around a little boy who was busy writing something. The 'wholeness' of the teahouse disappeared behind these specific people; what we had previously ignored came to the foreground. Every single table held a conference: whether it was two, three or even more people sitting around the table, they were all having a meeting while the people at the neighbouring table either attempted to eavesdrop or focus on the topics at their own 'conference'. There were as many topics as there were tables, just like a 'conversation expo'. The teahouse is not just theoretically categorised as a part of folk culture and folk customs, with teahouse conversations dubbed as noise of the masses; it is also a cultural phenomenon and a local feature. It is not just an experience for bystanders but also an object of cultural study for researchers.

The teahouse is like the Hive Theatre, with the simplest tables and chairs, their users constructing the boundaries and the content of the theatre. However, communications or, more specifically, conversations, constitute the basic rule. This rule, along with the table and chairs, turns into a tangible theatre. The theatre could be established with multiple 'stages'. In between the stages, the corridors and the use of the furniture (tables and chairs) divide up the 'performance' area into various sections. All sections are formed for the purpose of conversation. Each section has its own users, whose identities are erased and genders ignored, and who are simply treated as speakers and listeners. The speakers' voices, the content of their conversations, the ability to organise their words and their skills in attracting the temporary audience, are used in different sections at different times. It's like a drama performance that might pause at any time or sometimes even get interrupted by the audience; it's also like an arena where each speaker showcases their overall capability: can they introduce a new topic? Have they found an adjective that hits the nail on the head and even the pleasantness of their voice? Is there an appropriate person to top up the water and interrupt the conversation? Or perhaps the speaker picks up a phone call and has to leave, temporarily escaping from the embarrassment of an inappropriate use of words? If you imagine it as a family, they will replicate the scene of the whole family watching TV in the living room, post dinner. The most authoritative figure, sitting at the spot where the TV would be, may not be the eldest but is the most talkative. His role is to replace the very articulate news anchor that keeps talking on TV. Each 'stage' has its own logic of operation and keeps an appropriate distance from the neighbouring tables. Such distances hint at the tension of being simultaneously attracted to and isolated from one another. The tension leads to a kind of attentiveness which isn't planned by you but results from your being there.

Such attentiveness doesn't come wholeheartedly but is closer to reality. We may also say that we are living in the reality of collective action by the camera holder, the tape, the machine, the 'performers', the people looking at their phones, the people making noises and the audience. Every member of this reality, humans and nonhumans, are in an intense interaction with one another. We are not a 'sober' artist who is trying to collect images of a specific object, so as to transfer all the 'spoils' into a computer and produce something called 'artwork' through software. Instead, the work at hand needs to be reinterpreted – how is it different from 'existing work that has established its meaningfulness'?

The rapid switch between the baffling scene and the background does not surprise nor depress us. The background is always a blur, just like a dense jungle; an anxiety of not being in control. It is jumping between the familiar and the foreign.

Every hasty decision is perhaps a signal of 'losing control' that informs our body to embrace things unfamiliar to us, reminding us to be mindful that the sense of security that familiarity brings is fragile. At present, at this theatre (teahouse), there are no clear images or reassuring scenes. This means that, among these participants and the future, there are unknowns and things that will surprise me greatly.

Working with the machine and 'the others' is a type of physical therapy for me: to accept things as they are and not as they appear in our consciousness, to cast doubt on the confidence in our 'preconceptions'. We have mistaken the reality in our imagination as the true reality, hence we are unable to see things as they were. I have been replacing the true reality with my conscious judgement, thereby distancing myself further from reality.

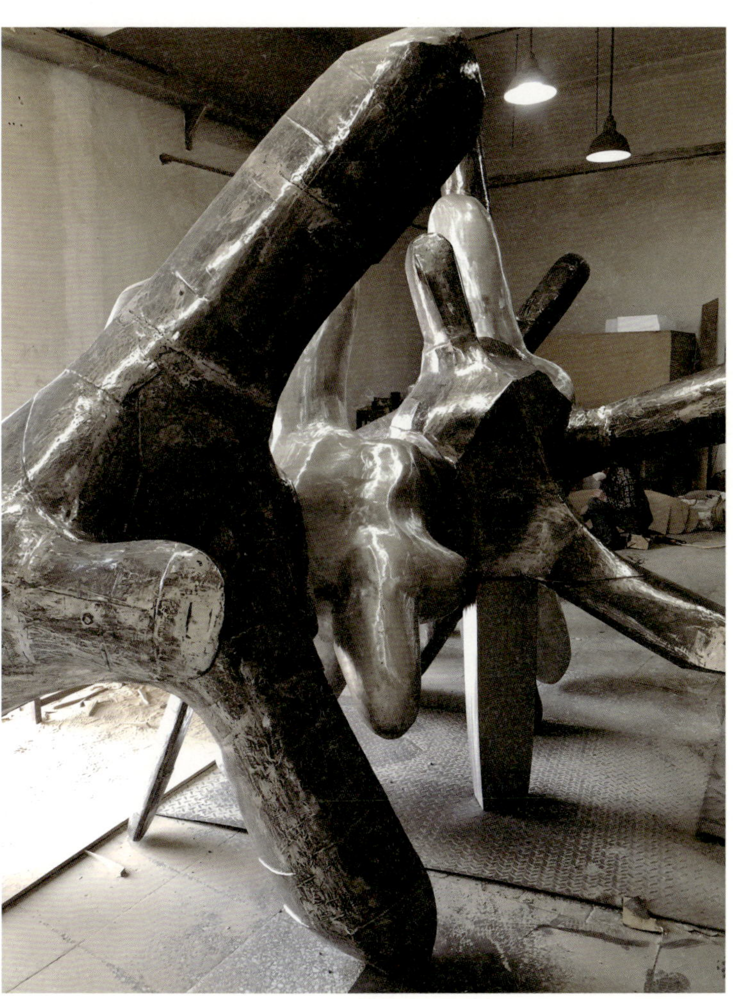

*What controls the ghostly quantum mechanics at ultra-far distances? Or is it the way it has always been? Physics took what was originally common for all living things and put it in its own pocket, turning it into an isolated area. The same happens to art.*

*What has turned into this thing called art? In the process of creating art, is it the result of the artist's complex hard work, the joyful projection of their bodies and minds forcing the materials to yield? In the process, the artist eliminates the 'inartistic' elements, cuts off unnecessary 'inartistic' branches, almost like a natural selection. According to this logic, art is only a shadow of certain human actions and, therefore, it is only with the creation of humans that art can follow as an attachment. However, according to the logic of biology, when there is only a single artist, he is unable to complete self-regulation and so the evolution of an individual does not exist in any sense. Such ability necessarily requires the interaction between him and the surrounding environment. Art originates from the fundamental biological mechanism of living things; it is a product of symbiosis of living things in a general sense.*

# TANGLE

At a crowded metro station exit, I don't notice the entire crowd but only one or a few in the crowd. How do they get picked from the crowd, or how are they freed from the cohort? Is it by chance? In any case, these few people and I establish a distance between the watched and the watching. Such a distance creates a space, which is not just confined to us but also among themselves, the stationary trains on the platform, and between the roof and the staircases. All these elements are part of the space. Therefore, beyond the connecting points and the vessel, space is an object full of possibilities that always generates 'more'.

A boy with a yellow cap appeared in my viewfinder. He had apparently come through a gap in the fence to a temporary construction site. To an analogue camera, the viewfinder established its own boundaries – its movement constantly cropped the real world into a world of its own and established its own site.

From the moment the boy entered the construction site, the viewfinder drew out a temporary boundary for the site. The machine seemed to have disconnected the construction site from the streets and turned it into a playground for the boy. He jumped into a trench, disappearing from the construction worker's view. He paused for a moment, savouring the joy of having escaped adults' watchful eyes. Then he walked around a pile of sand and stepped over some gravel. At this moment, he even slowed down and went to the blind spot of the viewfinder that had been following him. When he reappeared in the viewfinder, he turned out to be standing behind the cement mixer. The viewfinder and the boy moved around in two separate worlds defined by their own boundaries, yet they were tangled with each other: the viewfinder always tried to 'pre-empt' the boy's movement, so as to lock him inside the space reserved for him. Even though a human controlled the machine, he was just an assistant to the camera – it was the viewfinder that determined the position of the 'subject'. The real creator of the reality wasn't this boy either, but the construction site, the trench, the sand pile, the controller of the camera, the viewfinder and the construction worker, altogether. This is because, as time passed by, the boy's actions were bound by something else that was intangible – he was trying not to be seen by the construction worker, hence always bending down, a position that was in contrast with the construction worker's posture. The same space was divided into two sites by two different occupiers. Was it a construction site or a children's playground? The boy turned an actual construction site, or the part of the site that he explored, into a theatre; he even carved out a space of his own, in which common objects of a construction site, such as bricks, cement, pipes and gravel, were reorganised, dislocated, and their associations changed. The background of the construction site disappeared as the boy with the yellow cap took it into a moment that was 'unclear' (or inconclusive) while the viewfinder and I reconstructed a new sensory environment and image.

When we are confronted with the refusal of ordinary things, we discover their secrets that are otherwise difficult to unveil. Their refusal to compromise 'forces' us to pay greater attention to them and eventually realise that our preconception is flawed.

The key to discovering the secret, however, isn't self-reflection but the real contact we make with the external world.

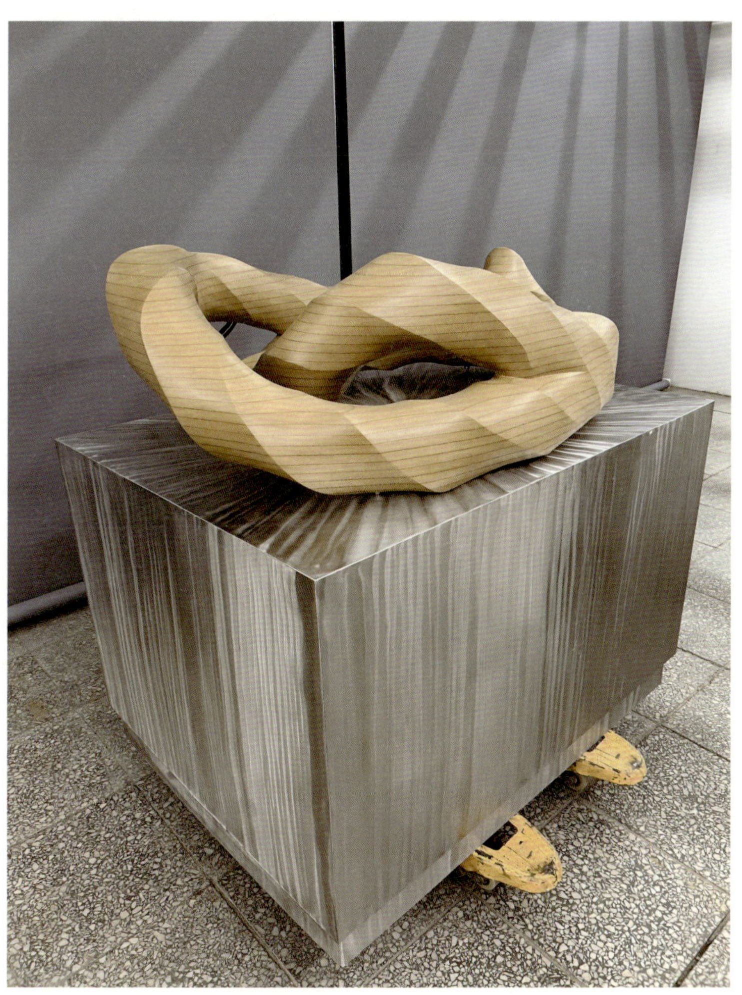

*The interests of life are not in things and are not in the 'self'. 'Self' is a space carved out by Modernism. It sits within itself, isolating its life from real life. Liberated from the Modernist theory, this master has turned into a slave of liberation.*

## METAPHOR

A TV was placed by the window with its back facing the street outside. Some pedestrians – visitors and tourists – were attracted by the faint image on the wall facing the TV through the glass window. They paused and pushed the door open. The faint image was a reflection of the TV screen. On TV, a video was playing repeatedly: a boy with a yellow cap was crossing a huge construction site. The site was fenced up with plastic sheets; outside the site was a street with people and cars passing by. The videographer apparently took the video from somewhere above the construction site. At this moment, every viewer 'naturally' assumed the position of the videographer and saw the boy pause, walk, step over different things – the obstacles in front of him: a newly dug-up trench, a concrete block, a pile of hot-rolled ribbed bars. He kept going, leaving a trail behind him but without a clear direction forward. The viewers joined the boy in his dilemma, which aroused their desire to help the boy imagine a route forward. At the same time, they were afraid of the boy making a wrong decision in his next step. Worry turned the viewing experience into a gaze and the viewers appeared to occupy two bodies: their actual body and the one gazing. The video transformed this moment into a real metaphor and the audience became part of this metaphorical theatre.

When they finished watching the video and pushed the door open again to leave, the TV was still on and the images retreated into the background of the TV. Alternatively, they were carried away by the audience.

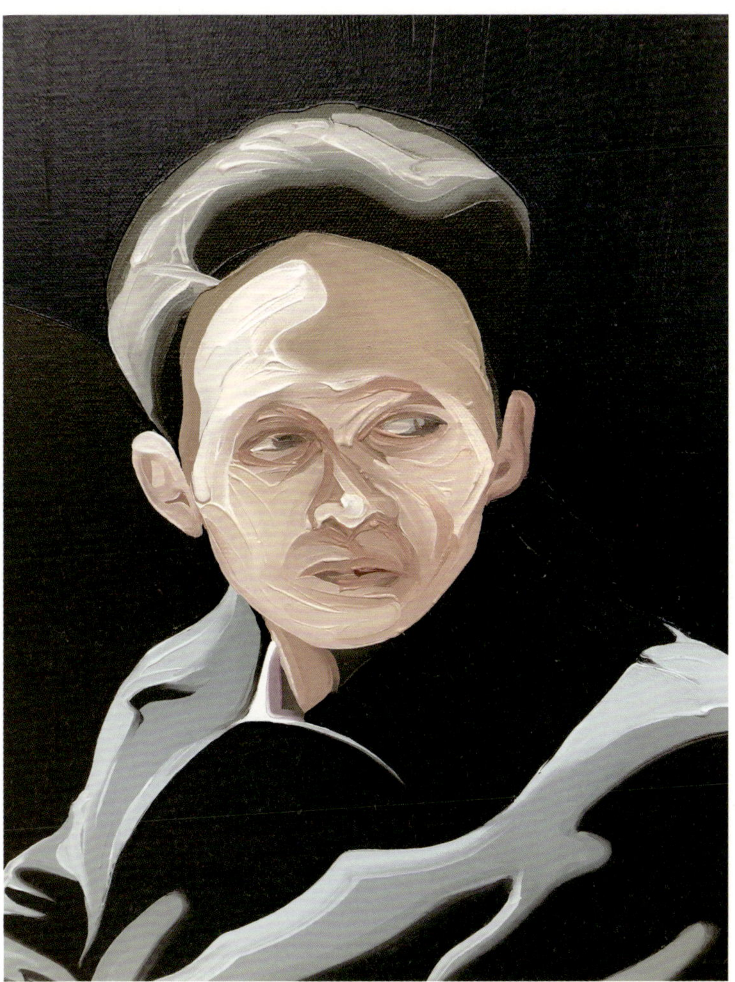

*The water in the environment is clear yet stinky. Microorganisms and oxygen constantly battle with each other. The battle is not intended as a show for human beings – they never care if human beings notice it, nor do they consciously avoid being seen by us. Things in the world cannot be restored by our knowledge alone. People who use knowledge are not free because we are all but products on the production line of Enlightenment.*

# CHAPTER 7

## STICKY

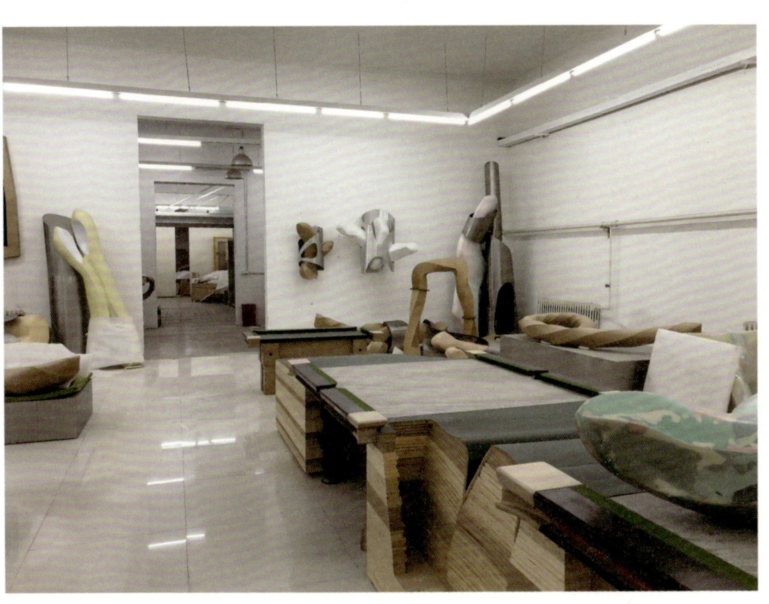

*Many things in the studio can be distinguished by size. For example, the building is large, the machines are smaller, and the tools are even smaller. Regardless of size, in flat ontology they can be said to exist in an asymmetric relationship with one another, representing an asymmetry between cognition and being.*

## FOREIGN SUBSTANCE

My mobile phone and I are in a symbiotic relationship: I have to rely on my phone and, thus, I am controlled by my phone; at the same time, it needs me for charging. The colour of the phone is the same as my body colour; the body of the phone is maintained by me. From this perspective, a painting seems like an animal domesticated by human and nonhuman. The mobile phone, the body, and the painting reposition the painting. According to Marshall McLuhan's theory of figure and ground, the mobile phone's intervention leads directly to a change of the drawing, its genetics even. The mobile phone changes the way the drawing was done, starting from the composition. In fact, the mobile phone fundamentally changes the artform of painting. The screens of mobile phones and computers, as well as canvases, form a new platform for painting. The nature and the working of this platform is just like stacking, not intended for restoration.

In paintings, stacking creates a vertical world. The generation, the source and the output of an image replace the concept, the composition and the technique. Such a geological practice naturally selects genetics that are in harmony with this new type of painting. Consequently, there will no longer be such a thing as 'one man's painting'; paintings are settled by my mobile phone and me. The collectivism of painting stems more from the participation of nonhumans. Screen, program, number, click, download, upload, crop, mix colour, choose canvas colour – always getting tangled into a collection of paintings. I have entered a construction site that consists of a certain infrastructure for the making of the painting: the foundation, construction, patterns, stacking of various materials. Or perhaps one becomes part of the scene for someone else. Painting puts me in a new environment whereby I am only a member of this collective activity.

In this activity, whether I like it or not, I am interacting with objects that I like and dislike. It's not up to me, although I am not entirely powerless.

My finger slides across the screen, defining my boundaries. On one hand, the establishment of boundaries depends on my technical capability – how much can I get out of it; on the other hand, it allows me to understand the content of the boundaries – my painting comes from a world of its own being while my phone and I turn this new world into a scene. I am an object and become part of a scene among various objects. I coexist with algae, reptiles, rocks and plants, all under the same roof. They gather together, according to the rules of things; humans no longer get to position animals, societies and histories into scenes. Every object appears in its own form with its own way of communicating, no longer representing the will of human beings. Neither are they symbolic – they are real objects as they truthfully exist in this 'flattened' world.

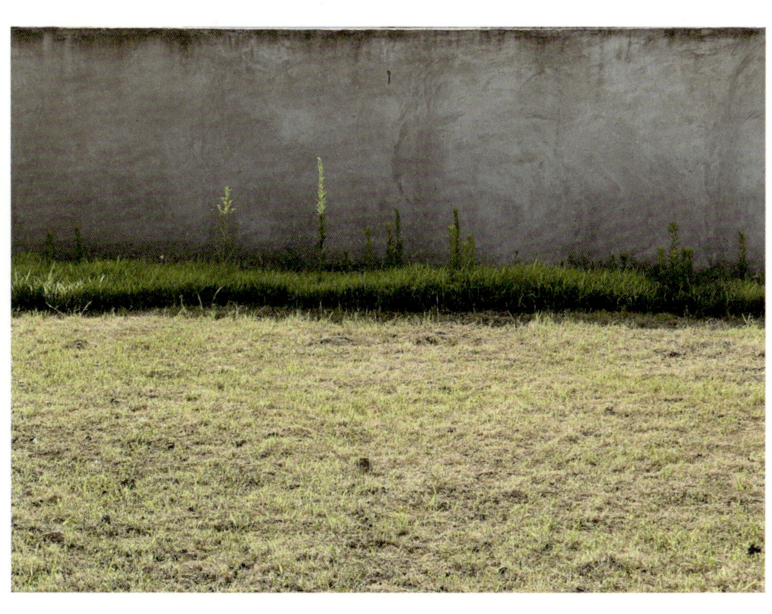

*I cannot impose the 'nature' of a noun on nature, for example, 'a lively tree'.*

# UNNATURAL

I see an image of a mountain and some plants on my computer screen, and they appear elongated. Maybe I was just looking at them objectively, trying to remember what they looked like in the moment. These plants and the mountain are glued together. I do not notice the mountain itself, the peak or the waterfalls; neither do I see the heavy structure, the multitude of colours or the natural environment in which the plants grow. Before 'restoring' their natural appearances, they present themselves differently to me. How did they get here? By algorithms or by computer programs? In any case, they do not appear as they would in their original habitat, but as a mountain on a screen, a medium within a medium – a new medium resulting from the crossover of a digital medium and nature. Besides, the modularisation of the mountain, the discord among the digital colours and the irregularity of the lines, make up the mountain that I see. I need to consider how to move it, how to remove it from the digital screen and let it exist in a new space. The mountain will be moved from one medium to another.

In fact, this action is done by the participant and his motivation. I am one of the participants, along with the mountain, the rocks, the roaming animals and fish, as well as many more plants, including their stems, branches and corolla. They are so ordinary, randomly arranged together; they come from a vast network and a narrowly defined reality. Yet, no matter where they come from, I can trace their lineage and learn the relevant knowledge. Their characteristics – colour, texture etc. – and their silhouettes can be dragged into this time and space. I don't know what other characteristics they have (soft, elastic, cold….) as I am unable to obtain them 'in their entirety'. Yet every single characteristic opens itself up to me, proving the power of its existence. I believe they are profound beyond understanding.

The profundity of each object allows me to 'more simply' ignore some characteristics, which in turn affects my immersion in those objects.

This is true for the 'growth' of a sculpture. At first, what I can see and touch are just pieces of OSB. I have a very simple and objective view of the materials – they are glued together layer by layer, not requiring any special technique or treatment as it's just 'a pile' of OSB. I am not sure how this 'pile' will evolve. I only know that any change would require a new 'participant'. The electric saw and the electric hammer are the first participants to modify the geometric shape, allowing the pile to escape from its initially distinguishable cubic shape. Using such a process to blur its shape isn't simple. As it's a collective of multiple 'participants', I need to first change my 'mind', which is at this moment just one of the participants. Limitation begins with the imagination of the artist as well as his decisiveness, because other 'participants' are collectively constructing a new environment in their own way. In this environment, apart from me, there are other tools – the electric hammer and the electric saw, as well as the electricity, the air pressure and the temperature that are all actively at play in the background.

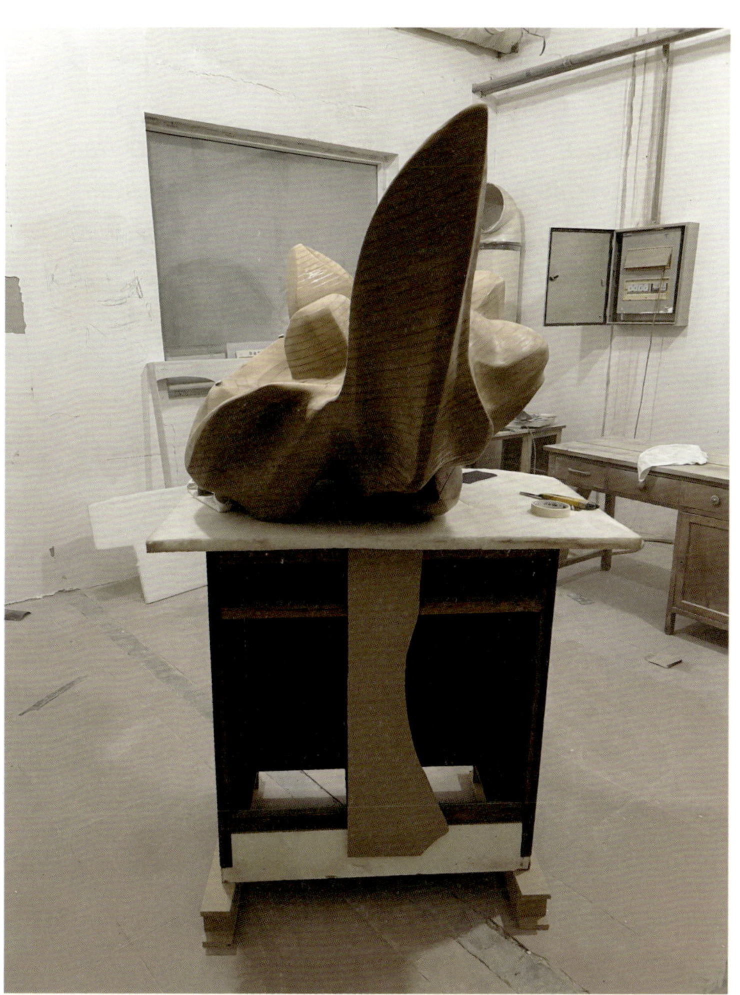

*Take the example of a budding plant: its entire life is a history of adventure. Apart from inheriting genes, it needs to exist not just for survival but to keep evolving. An object only lives on as such.*

# ANIMALS

An organism is able to recognise things around it as much as possible, while communicating with, relying on and escaping from the environment. It has an inborn ability to perceive. Artists do not require any special training to attain this ability as it is part of their biological function. Along with movement, consideration, judgement and action, the ability to perceive helps generate so-called 'thought'. Thought is the result of an interaction between an organism and its environment. This is perhaps why the original impulse of art is destined not to be a moral choice or to have its roots in humanism, but to come from a biological inclination. Before human beings singled them out as ‘thoughts’, they were simply serving the purpose of life.

We have only obtained the manual and the user guide for life. All images of life are stored in the vast universe. Organisms then identify these images. Such an ability stems from the functioning of a certain nervous system to sense some sort of ‘wonder’. From this perspective, judgements on art are not based on, but are beyond experience – only when taken out of context, is the relationship between art and the organic nature of life more convincing. Therefore, ‘wonder’ doesn’t just cover aesthetics, but also the ignorance that makes people ‘wonder’. We all inherit some kind of characteristic of an organism to different extents. Such characteristics used to have distinct features but are now drowned in textbooks and historical knowledge. Wang Guowei’s judgement of truth stemmed from this. To him, subjectivists seek truth from within and, thus, truth is a result of the operation of the nervous system. Even though it is difficult to judge, truth exists. The British painter Francis Bacon was of the same opinion. In this light, art is not a tool to create any ‘meaning’ (celebration, praise, revelation, critique, truth, order....); it merely functions like a bacterium – an ancient form of life – to self-generate. Art is a phenomenon that results from biological evolution – it is common among all living things on Earth and can be interpreted in a larger reality. No matter how art is explained and categorised in textbooks, the biological explanation cannot be excluded.

The biological features of art come from the self-reflection of organisms as a form of self-generation in the general sense. Bernard Stiegler's view was that technology and tools (those we already have and those to be invented) help externalise this action. Such organic knowledge has become a fundamental feature of modern society.

Artists maintain themselves through changes or by paying attention to changes. This process is full of control and chaos – some are seen, understood (either beforehand or afterwards) and sensed. These tangible but unspeakable things change our objects. No single factor can determine what can or cannot be seen. It is a more universal kind of behaviour. Alternatively, we could say it's an approach whereby many more things that are yet to be identified are involved. This is probably the most common situation I face. At the same time, this universality also means it doesn't come from one particular source, such as art, honour or power. Just like endorphins are a result of evolution, the ability to perceive the external environment is a biological feature of the nervous system. That is to say, the so-called 'individualisation' never means separation – 'thoughts' and bodies both come about as a result of perception by organisms. So-called aesthetics, joy, intuition, judgement, what we already know, what we can learn, perhaps all result from biological evolution, and not any concept.

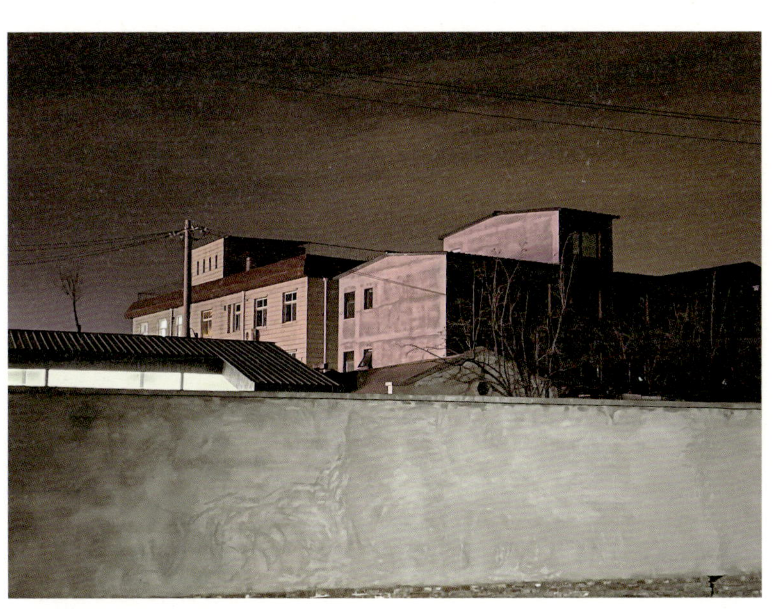

*History is definitely not built with 'bright things', but with true darkness that cannot even be reached through knowledge. Every single past that we made use of is just another raw material for our action.*

# EPILOGUE

Even before a sculpture was displayed on the exhibition table or a painting in an art space, what I call 'materials' already existed. Their existence came before the artworks, it's just that I was not looking at them.

I only invoked some of the objects that I worked with in order to demonstrate the reality of the environment – messy and uncertain.

The content of each subheading is a gathering in a messy situation. Apart from the main theme, which requires no necessary explanation, there is no coherent logic to these subheadings. Very often, different elements may not present the same effect; they could even be in conflict. This is another fundamental characteristic of the 'flattened' world today – we rely on each other, fight with each other, but also become entangled with one another and, as such, give rise to wondrous ambiguities.

All pictures here provide some clue in parallel. They are neither intended as clarification for words, nor presented separately as unique scenes. Just like me, they are invoked here as part of a collective. I hope I have paid due respect to the collective that I have worked with, not just out of courtesy but also because I am nervous about my narratives – no matter what I have said, they cannot be refuted. On the contrary, this was a test for my consciousness, ethics and rhetoric – more or less.

ISBN: 978-1-78884-290-7

Published by ACC Art Books in association with Guangxi Normal University Press 2025



A CIP catalogue record for this book is available from the British Library

Editors: Alice Bowden, Ru Jingyu
Designer: Fiona Liu (Jian Feng)

Printed in China
for ACC Art Books Ltd., Woodbridge, Suffolk, UK

www.accartbooks.com
www.gxnu.edu.cn

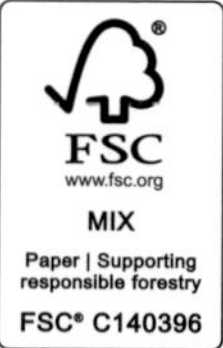


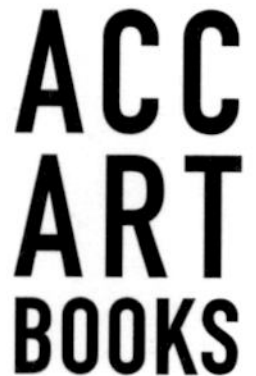